F·R·I·E·N·D·S

THE TELEVISION SERIES

The Official Cookbook

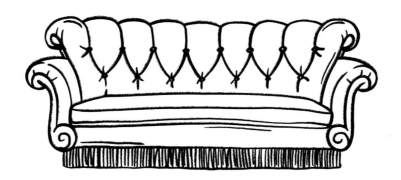

F·R·I·E·N·D·S

THE TELEVISION SERIES

The Official Cookbook

WRITTEN BY **AMANDA YEE**

INSIGHT EDITIONS

San Rafael • Los Angeles • London

Contents

Main Dishes

Dinner With Friends

Sweets and Desserts

Drinks

F·R·I·E·N·D·S

Introduction

There's no denying that food is a huge part of the *Friends* universe. Sure, we can all remember Rachel's meat trifle, but can you recall an episode with Joey in it where he isn't eating? Would it have been funny enough if Ross's intestinal issues were caused by something other than eating dodgy tacos? What if Monica were a dentist?

As we watch and re-watch the episodes, we begin to understand that the sharing of meals together perfectly encapsulates how food is one of the unifying things that builds a community. If not in New York City, where else could one get authentic rice and gandules or zongzi within a 300 mile radius? And who else would one share those treasures with if not one's neighbors, coffeehouse acquaintances, and fellow subway commuters?

Ross, Monica, Chandler, Joey, Phoebe, and Rachel's stories sprung to life in a New York City ripe with fresh ideas, multiple cultures, and untapped potential to set the scene. It is the evergreen timelessness and relatability of the stories woven around eating that stay with fans around the globe. From wearing a Thanksgiving turkey on Joey and Monica's head to the importance of *unagi*, fans of *Friends* everywhere can relate to the trials and tribulations of trying to make it in the world in their 20s and 30s.

Much like the characters in *Friends*, I built worthy connections within my community by saying hi to my neighbors when we were both in the hallway. I offered help if I saw them struggling to carry their packages up the stairs. I smiled. Eventually, I did the only thing that made sense to me at the time: I invited my neighbors over for a shared meal. I can't remember what I cooked that day when 15 people were piled into my tiny apartment, but the one thing I do remember is that the people who attended that dinner are still some of my most valued and trusted friends to date.

As such, I've made many of the recipes in this cookbook large enough to share with friends and family. The recipes also reflect each of the Friends' (and many side characters') personal tastes. Some of Monica's recipes reflect her abilities as a chef, some of Rachel's recipes feature fancier ingredients based on her upper-crust background, and Joey's recipes are delicious crowd-pleasers. Though each recipe is different, they are all meant to bring people together in order to enjoy each other's company.

My hope for this cookbook is that it not only emboldens our love for *Friends*, but in the philosophies inherent in the series. These philosophies are what make the show worthy of nostalgia: May we extend grace and forgiveness to one another like Rachel and Ross; may we extend generosity to one another like Chandler and Joey (except when it comes to food: Joey doesn't share food!); may we extend loyalty like Monica, and sincerity and laughter like Phoebe. Most of all, may we extend the pleasure of eating together and the sharing of a meal with friends.

— Amanda Yee

Monica's
Blue Cupboard Basics

Every good home cook or chef has a repertoire of spreads, sauces, jams, and stocks from which they can build many delicious meals and feasts for loved ones, family, and friends. Monica's well-stocked blue cupboard was a lifesaver anytime an extra food-loving friend showed up unannounced or when she needed to throw Rachel a going-away party. Having these items on hand will turn simple meals into fun, memorable feasts. Just make sure to clean and dust the top of your canned jar lids every once in a while or, if you're anything like Monica, a lot!

Rapini Pesto, the Best-O

Ham Spread

Ranch BBQ Sauce

Cumin Chili Ketchup

Pie Crust

The Opposite of Man: Blackberry Mint Jam

Lemon Curd

Turkey Stock

Vegetable Stock

Pickled Red Onion

Crispy Shallots

Rapini Pesto, the Best-O

When Phoebe goes to the kitchen at Monica's restaurant, it's not clear whether the cute new sous-chef Tim's pesto is "the best-o" or just "pretty good-o," but when Monica says she wants to fire him because he's not good at the job, the quality of his pesto can't save him. This pesto though, made with rapini, also known as broccoli rabe, is definitely the best-o.

1 bunch rapini
½ cup dry-roasted almonds
Zest and juice of 1 lemon
⅓ cup grated Pecorino Romano cheese
⅓ cup extra-virgin olive oil
Salt and pepper

In a food processor, combine the rapini, almonds, lemon zest and juice, and cheese and pulse to combine. With the processor running, slowly drizzle in olive oil until a paste forms. Season with salt and pepper to taste. Cover and refrigerate for up to 2 weeks.

Ham Spread

⅓ cup Calabrian chile peppers
 in oil
½ cup cubed guanciale or
 pancetta
⅓ cup red wine
½ pound sliced salami
2 tablespoons olive oil
¼ cup (½ stick) butter
Salt and pepper

Remove the stems from the peppers and separate from the oil. Set the oil aside and place peppers in a food processor.

Add the guanciale or pancetta, red wine, salami, olive oil, and butter to the food processor and pulse until a thick paste forms, about 5 to 7 minutes.

While the paste is pulsing, slowly drizzle in the reserved chile oil. Season with salt and pepper to taste. Cover and refrigerate for up to 2 weeks.

A NOTE FROM CHEF MONICA: This recipe calls for Calabrian chile peppers in oil. It's highly recommended that you use these flavorful chiles, but if you need a substitute you can use another chile such as Fresno or poblano and a separate chile oil but the flavor will be quite different.

Ranch BBQ Sauce

YIELD: 4 servings
PREP TIME: 5 minutes
INACTIVE TIME: 2 to 4 hours

½ cup full-fat buttermilk
½ cup crème fraîche or sour cream
3 tablespoons mayonnaise
2 tablespoons dried dill
1 tablespoon garlic powder
1 tablespoon onion powder
¼ cup minced fresh chives
2 tablespoons Worcestershire sauce
1 tablespoon white vinegar
Salt and pepper
2 tablespoons prepared
   barbecue sauce

In a large bowl, combine the buttermilk, crème fraiche or sour cream, mayonnaise, dill, garlic powder, onion powder, chives, Worcestershire sauce, and vinegar. Stir until the ingredients are well incorporated. Season to taste with salt and pepper. Cover and refrigerate for 2 to 4 hours.

Before serving, stir in the barbecue sauce. Add more to your liking. Cover and refrigerate for up to 1 week.

Cumin Chili Ketchup

YIELD: 4 servings
PREP TIME: 5 minutes

1 tablespoon ground cumin
1½ tablespoons chili powder
Zest and juice of 1 lime
10 ounces prepared ketchup
Salt and pepper

In a small bowl, mix together the cumin, chili powder, lime zest and juice, and ketchup. Season with salt and pepper to taste. Store in an airtight container in the refrigerator for up to two weeks.

Pie Crust

YIELD: 2 pie crusts
PREP TIME: 20 minutes
INACTIVE TIME: 1 hour

This pie crust recipe includes thyme that will complement any savory pie. For a sweet pie dough, omit the thyme, or if you'd like to experiment, try a different herb.

2¼ cups all-purpose flour
1 teaspoon sugar
1 teaspoon salt
1 cup (2 sticks) unsalted butter, frozen and cut into pea-size cubes
¼ cup fresh thyme, stemmed
⅓ cup ice-cold water
1 tablespoon apple cider vinegar

In a large bowl, stir together the flour, sugar, and salt.

Spread the small cubes of butter around the flour in the bowl and stir to coat. Once cubes are coated, using your forefinger and thumb, rub the cubes until they become flat and coated with flour. Gently stir cubes into the flour, but do not mix.

Sprinkle the thyme evenly over the dough.

Make a well in the middle of the mixture, and slowly add in 1 tablespoon of water at a time. Begin to fold the dough together, being careful not to overwork or overmix. The dough should start to stick together, after about 30 to 40 seconds. Add the apple cider vinegar, and continue to mix until dough is well mixed and smooth, about 1 to 3 minutes.

If the dough is still a bit dry, add in ½ teaspoon of cold water at a time, while mixing.

Once dough is smooth, wrap in plastic wrap, and refrigerate for at least 1 hour.

The Opposite of Man: Blackberry Mint Jam

What's the opposite of "man"? Jam! Or so Monica says when she makes a metric ton of jam in an attempt to get over Richard. Serve with Jam-and-a-Spoon Scones (page 147).

5 cups blackberries
3 tablespoons dried mint
Zest and juice of 1 lemon
2½ cups sugar
2 tablespoons bourbon (optional)

Combine all the ingredients in a large pot. Turn the heat to medium-low and allow ingredients to thicken, stirring occasionally, 20 to 30 minutes.

Once thick, pour the jam into sterilized canning jars, leaving about ½ inch of headspace. Allow to cool to room temperature, then cover and store in the refrigerator for up to 1 week.

Lemon Curd

⅔ cup sugar
4 egg yolks
Zest and juice of 2 or 3 small lemons
6 tablespoons (¾ stick) butter

In a small bowl, whisk together the sugar and the yolks until mixture becomes a pale yellow, about 2 minutes. Add the lemon zest and juice, and stir until well incorporated, about 1 minute.

Heat a medium saucepan on low heat, and transfer the egg mixture into the pan. Stirring vigorously, begin to add pads of butter until the mixture thickens and forms a curd, 6 to 7 minutes. Once thickened, remove from the heat, allow to cool, and store in refrigerator for up to 1 week.

Turkey Stock

YIELD: 1½ liters
COOK TIME: 3½ hours

Making stock is a great way to limit food waste. It is recommended that you use a combination of herbs, vegetables, and even some fruits that are on the verge of going to waste. What's important for a meat-based stock is that in conjunction with leftover fruits, veggies, and herbs, you use the bones of the animal.

1 turkey carcass
2 onions, peeled and halved
4 celery stalks, cut to fit in the pot
4 large carrots, cut to fit in the pot
2 tablespoons pink peppercorns
3 to 4 bay leaves
1 bunch parsley
Salt and pepper

Combine all the ingredients except salt and pepper in a large pot and fill with water until the ingredients are submerged, leaving 1 to 2 inches of headspace. Cover and bring to a boil over medium-high heat.

Reduce heat to medium-low and allow to simmer uncovered for 2 to 3 hours, until stock has reduced somewhat. Strain and discard the solids, and season the stock with salt and pepper to taste.

If not using immediately, transfer to portion-sized freezer-safe containers with the lids off. Allow the stock to come to room temperature before covering and freezing.

Vegetable Stock

YIELD: 1½ liters
COOK TIME: 3½ hours

2 onions, peeled and halved
2 celery stalks, cut to fit in the pot
4 large carrots, cut to fit in the pot
2 lemons, halved
½ pound mushrooms (any kind, including woody stems)
½ pound tomatoes
4 potatoes, quartered
1 to 2 bunches herbs
Salt and pepper

Combine all the ingredients except salt and pepper in a large pot and fill with water until the ingredients are fully submerged, leaving 1 to 2 inches of headspace. Cover and bring to a boil over medium-high heat.

Reduce heat to medium-low and allow to simmer uncovered for 2 to 3 hours, until stock has reduced. Strain and discard the solids, and season the stock with salt and pepper to taste.

If not using immediately, transfer to portion-sized freezer-safe containers with the lids off. Allow the stock to come to room temperature before covering and freezing.

A NOTE FROM CHEF MONICA: You can use any vegetables in this recipe, including trimmings from vegetables you would have originally discarded. Some options you can use include: Woody mushroom stems, any sort of tomatoes, unused herb stems, and more.

Pickled Red Onion

YIELD: 2 servings
PREP TIME: 5 minutes
INACTIVE TIME: 8 hours

1 large red onion, sliced
1 tablespoon cumin seeds
3 to 4 bay leaves
1 cup apple cider vinegar
½ cup sugar
½ cup salt

Place the red onion, cumin, and bay leaves in a jar with a tight-fitting lid.

In a small bowl, mix together apple cider vinegar, sugar, and salt until well combined, about 2 minutes.

Pour the vinegar mixture over the onions until the liquid reaches the brim of the jar. Use a folded piece of parchment paper to weigh the onions down, if they poke up through the liquid.

Cover and allow to marinate, refrigerated, overnight before using. Onions can be kept for up to 3 weeks.

Crispy Shallots

YIELD: 1 serving
PREP TIME: 25 minutes

½ cup coconut oil or vegetable oil
1 large shallot, cut into thin rings
Salt and pepper

Heat a large pot or a wok on medium-high. Add the oil, and heat until it reaches 300°F.

Add the shallots and give it a stir. Once the shallots begin to bubble, about 5 minutes, turn the heat down to medium-low. Fry the shallots for 15 to 18 minutes, stirring occasionally, until crispy and browned.

Using a slotted spoon, scoop out the shallots and place on a plate lined with a paper towel. Season with salt and pepper to taste.

"Alright,
what are we havin'?"

—Joey

Breakfast

Marcel's Nutty Chocolatey Cakey French Toast Thing
(Stuffed French Toast)

Rachel's Dried Fruit and Granola Parfait

Phoebe's Post-Run Recovery Bars

Janice's Oh. My. Gawd. Pancakes

Morning's Here Bagels

Eggs à la Chandler

Ross's Chilaquiles

1950s Diner Special: Gentlemen Prefer
Breakfast Sausage and Gravy

Marcel's Nutty Chocolatey Cakey French Toast Thing
(Stuffed French Toast)

YIELD:
6 to 8 servings

PREP AND COOK TIME:
35 minutes

To compensate for his ex-wife leaving him for another woman, Ross does the natural thing and gets a Capuchin monkey named Marcel. Is life finding you a little down and out? Instead of getting an exotic pet, try self-soothing the delicious banana-y and chocolatey way—eat French toast with friends! Believe me, French toast is your best choice. French toast never hits puberty, and you never have to worry about it doing questionable things to your stuffed animals.

2 large loaves challah bread, cut into 3-inch-thick slices
8 ounces mascarpone cheese
¼ cup confectioners' sugar
3 tablespoons unsweetened cocoa powder
Pinch of sea salt
1 cup heavy whipping cream
1 cup milk
1 tablespoon ground cinnamon
1 tablespoon vanilla extract
4 large eggs
Zest of ½ orange
Cooking spray
½ cup smoked almonds, measured and roughly chopped, for serving
3 large bananas, sliced into 1-inch rounds, for serving
Maple or chocolate syrup, for serving

A NOTE FROM CHEF MONICA: To pipe the filling, use a piping bag or a large plastic zip-top bag with a corner cut off. Place a piping tip inside of the bag, and place the bag in a large container. Secure the edges of the bag to the container. Scoop the mixed ingredients into the piping bag. Once placed in the bag, tightly twist the top of the bag to secure.

Working lengthwise, make a 2-inch slit about ½-inch deep in the crust of each slice of bread.

In a medium bowl, whisk together the mascarpone cheese, confectioners' sugar, and cocoa powder until well combined, 1 to 2 minutes. Add a pinch of sea salt to taste.

Fit a piping bag with a piping tip or prepare a large plastic zip-top bag with a corner cut off and fill it with the mascarpone mixture. Gently squeeze a small amount of the mascarpone mixture into a bread slit until bread cavity is filled. (Don't overstuff, otherwise it will leave a big mess when the toast is cooking.) Set aside on a baking tray. Repeat with the remaining bread slices.

In a separate medium bowl, combine the heavy whipping cream, milk, cinnamon, vanilla, eggs, and orange zest until well incorporated, about 1 to 2 minutes.

Place a large skillet or nonstick pan on medium heat and spray the pan with cooking spray. Working in batches, dip the stuffed bread into the egg mixture until well covered, but not soggy, on both sides. Once adequately soaked, place 1 or 2 slices of stuffed bread in pan.

Allow the bread to crisp up, 2 to 3 minutes, and then flip to crisp on other side. The bread should be soft and firm to the touch, but no longer wet. Once done, place on a serving tray lined with paper towels and repeat until all slices are cooked.

Serve topped with smoked almonds, banana slices, and your favorite maple or chocolate syrup.

Rachel's Dried Fruit and Granola Parfait

YIELD: 6 servings
PREP AND COOK TIME: 50 minutes

It's not a secret that Rachel has a huge crush on her assistant, Tag, even though she goes to great lengths to hide it from her coworkers. When she's caught sniffing the sweater he left in his backpack, she makes a supersmooth recovery and says she's just going to fill "her" backpack with, you know, granola and dried fruit. Totally normal and casual! This parfait is a little fancier than Rachel might have had in mind but will definitely help cover up any forbidden office crushes.

GRANOLA:
1 cup raw almonds
½ cup sunflower seeds
⅓ cup dried blueberries
⅓ cup dried cranberries
½ cup maple syrup
½ cup coconut oil, melted,
  or canola oil
1 tablespoon ground cinnamon
4 cups oats
Sea salt

PARFAIT:
12 ounces Greek yogurt
Lemon Curd (page 13)
Fresh berries (optional)

TO MAKE THE GRANOLA:
Preheat the oven to 375°F and line a baking sheet with parchment paper.

In a large bowl, mix together all the ingredients, making sure that the oats are evenly coated with both oil and maple syrup.

Evenly spread the oat mixture over the prepared baking sheet and bake until granola is dry, golden, and clumpy, about 10 minutes. Allow to cool for about 30 minutes.

TO MAKE THE PARFAIT:
Place a generous amount of Greek yogurt in the bottom of a bowl. Top with an even and generous layer of lemon curd, and finish with granola and fresh berries, if using.

Phoebe's Post-Run Recovery Bars

Season 6, Episode 7
"The One Where Phoebe Runs"

YIELD: 12 bars
PREP TIME: 40 minutes
INACTIVE TIME: 4 hours

When Rachel moves in with Phoebe, they decide to do more things with one another. On their first run together through Central Park, Rachel discovers that Phoebe runs like a flailing five-year-old and is embarrassed to be seen with her. Phoebe, on the other hand, is ecstatic and excited about running. We can only imagine how tired and in need of recovery Phoebe might be after running through the park. If you'd like to recover from doing your own version of Phoebe's run, try these recovery bars—they're packed with protein and antioxidants, and are low in sugar.

3 to 5 pitted dates
¼ cup water
¼ cup almond butter
1 tablespoon coconut oil
3 tablespoons vanilla pea protein
¼ cup chocolate chips
3 tablespoons dried blueberries
1 cup cooked quinoa
1¼ cup oats
Cooking spray

In a blender on high speed, combine the dates and water. Blend for 3 to 4 minutes, until the dates are dissolved. Set aside.

In a medium bowl, mix together the almond butter, coconut oil, and pea protein until well incorporated. Add the date and water mixture, and stir vigorously until the almond butter mixture is still thick, but a bit runny, 3 to 4 minutes.

Add the chocolate chips, dried blueberries, quinoa, and oats. Stir until mixture thickens, about 2 minutes

Coat an 8-inch baking pan with cooking spray.

Using a rubber spatula, scoop bar mixture evenly into baking pan, patting firmly down to avoid lumps. Place in a freezer for at least 4 hours or overnight.

Once frozen, cut into your desired shape, and enjoy after running like a wild woman through Central Park.

"Come on!
That's not running, let's go!"

—Phoebe

Janice's Oh. My. Gawd. Pancakes

YIELD:
2 to 3 servings

PREP AND COOK TIME:
40 minutes

Oh. My. Gawd. The soft, cloudlike texture of these pancakes is more intense than Janice's love for Chandler Bing! But Chandler generally doesn't want to share the air Janice breathes. Oblivious to his indifference, Janice believes Chandler is her soul mate. Then one day, in a stunning change of heart, Chandler begins to fall in love with Janice. Instead of rushing her out the door, Chandler lets her stay, and she makes pancakes!

½ teaspoon ground cinnamon

1 vanilla bean pod, scraped, or 1 teaspoon vanilla extract

1 cup ricotta cheese

Zest and juice of 1 lemon

2 tablespoons muscovado sugar or granulated sugar

¾ cup milk

2 large eggs, beaten

1 cup all-purpose flour

1 teaspoon baking powder

Butter or cooking spray

1 cup fresh berries, for serving (optional)

Warm maple syrup, for serving

In a large bowl, combine the cinnamon, vanilla, ricotta, lemon zest and juice, sugar, milk, and eggs. Stir until well incorporated, 2 to 3 minutes.

Sift together the all-purpose flour and baking powder, and gently fold into the wet batter.

Heat a large pan on high. Once hot, reduce the heat to medium-low and add butter or cooking spray to the pan. Working in batches, gently scoop about a half cup of batter per pancake into the pan and allow to bubble, 2 to 3 minutes. Once bubbly, flip the pancakes and cook until done, 2 to 3 minutes longer. Set on a warm plate and repeat with the remaining batter.

Serve with fresh berries and warm maple syrup.

"Monica and Rachel had syrup. Now I can get my man to cheer up!"

—Janice

23

Morning's Here Bagels

YIELD:
12 bagels

**PREP AND
COOK TIME:**
3½ hours

INACTIVE TIME:
30 minutes

"Morning's here! The morning's here! Sunshine is here! The sky is clear. Our morning's here! Go get into gear . . ." Bagels for breakfast are here! Rachel wasn't a fan of her chipper neighbor's morning habit of loudly singing his made-up song, and it was enough to convince her that she and Monica needed to switch their apartments back with Joey and Chandler. If she had these savory breakfast bagels to look forward to, she might have had a completely different opinion on mornings!

1¼ cup lukewarm water, divided
1½ ounces fresh yeast
1 teaspoon granulated sugar
4 cups high-protein bread flour
2 teaspoons salt
4 tablespoons brown sugar, divided
Oil, for bowl

In a small bowl, combine the lukewarm water with the yeast and granulated sugar. Allow to sit until the yeast becomes frothy, 1 to 2 minutes.

In the bowl of a stand mixer fitted with a dough hook, or in a large bowl if kneading by hand, combine the yeast mixture with the additional 1 cup water, flour, salt, and 2 tablespoons of the brown sugar, and mix on medium-low speed. Allow to mix for 10 minutes (15 to 20 minutes if by hand). The dough is done kneading when it slaps against the side of the mixing bowl and doesn't lose its shape. If kneading by hand, the dough should be tense, but quite smooth.

Place the dough in a well-oiled bowl, set in a warm place (on top of a refrigerator works), cover, and allow to rise for 90 minutes.

Line two baking sheets with parchment paper. Place the dough on a nonporous work surface and divide into 12 pieces. Roll the dough into balls (no extra flour is necessary) and place on the prepared baking sheets. Cover and allow the balls to rest for 20 to 30 minutes.

Preheat the oven to 425°F. Fill a large pot three-quarters of the way with water, add the remaining 2 tablespoons brown sugar, and heat on medium-high. Allow the water to come to a boil.

Using your index finger, poke a hole in the middle of a dough ball, and give the dough a spin on your finger, until the hole is about 1½ inches in diameter. Repeat with all of the dough balls.

Working in batches, place 2 to 3 bagels face down in the boiling water for 1 to 2 minutes, until they rise to the surface of the water. Using a spider strainer or a slotted spoon, flip bagels after they have risen. Cook for 1 to 2 minutes longer, then remove from the water and place on the baking sheets.

Bake for 15 to 20 minutes, until the bagels are golden brown. Be sure to rotate the baking sheets about 12 minutes into baking to ensure even browning.

Bagel variations continued on the next page . . .

Bagel Variations:

SPICED OR HERBED BAGELS:

1 egg white
1 tablespoon water
Dried herbs or spices of your choice

If you'd like to add delicious spices or dried herb toppings to your bagel, beat 1 egg white and 1 tablespoon water together. Remove the bagels from oven about 10 minutes into baking, and brush each bagel with egg white mixture. Sprinkle herbs on top of the bagel, and return to the oven to finish baking.

JALAPENO CHEESE BAGELS:

Monterey Jack or cheddar cheese
Pickled or fresh jalapeno, diced

Sprinkle shredded Monterey Jack or cheddar cheese on top of the bagels 10 minutes into baking. Return to oven. Once the cheese is melted, 2 to 3 minutes, place slices of pickled or fresh jalapeno on the cheese, and finish baking. The cheese should be bubbly and light brown in some spots.

LOADED SAVORY BAGELS:

8 ounces (1 package) cream cheese, at room temperature
1 bunch chives, finely chopped
Salt and pepper
1 large beefsteak tomato, sliced into ¼-inch-thick rounds
1 large cucumber, sliced into rounds
1 large red onion, cut into rings
One 4-ounce jar capers, drained
12 ounces cured salmon
4 to 6 ounces sprouts of your choice (such as alfalfa or pea shoots)
Fried eggs (optional)

In a small bowl with a whisk, or using a hand mixer, whip together cream cheese and chives until incorporated. Season with salt and pepper to taste. Cut the fresh, warm bagels open with a bread knife. Smear cream cheese on both sides of the bagel then layer on tomato, cucumber, red onion, and capers. Top with salmon and sprouts, and fried eggs, if using.

SWEET BAGELS:

8 ounces (1 package) cream cheese, at room temperature
3 tablespoons The Opposite of Man: Blackberry Mint Jam (page 13) or your favorite store-bought jam
8 to 12 large strawberries or berries of your choice, sliced in order to lay flat

In a small bowl with a whisk, or using a hand mixer, whip together the cream cheese and jam, then smear the cream cheese mixture on both sides of a bagel. Top with sliced strawberries. Sing "Morning's here!" between bites.

Eggs à la Chandler

Season 2, Episode 17
"The One Where Eddie Moves In"

YIELD: 4 servings
PREP AND COOK TIME: 20 minutes

Nobody likes two different kinds of eggs equally, or so Joey says indignantly after he discovers Chandler enjoying his eggs à la Eddie. He probably should have thought of this before he moved out and Eddie moved in with Chandler! Since we all know that the only eggs Chandler ever needs are made by Joey—with the bread, with the hole in the middle—this is Chandler's version, but with a little pesto added as a nod to Eddie.

4 slices sourdough bread,
    cut into 2-inch slices
2 tablespoons unsalted butter
4 eggs
Salt and pepper
2 tablespoons Rapini Pesto, the
    Best-O (page 10) or store-bought
    pesto

Using a cookie cutter or a small round dish, cut a hole in each slice of bread about 3 inches in diameter.

Heat a large pan on high. While it heats, evenly butter a slice of bread on both sides. Once hot, reduce the heat to medium and place the bread in the pan. Place a bit of butter in the hole of the toast and crack an egg into the hole. Allow the egg to cook, about 1 minute. Flip and cook the toast and egg to the desired consistency, 1 to 3 minutes. Remove from the heat and set aside. Salt and pepper to taste. Repeat with the remaining bread and eggs.

Drizzle with pesto and serve.

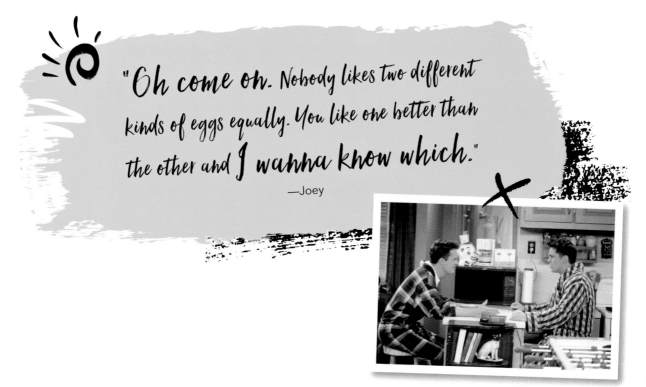

"Oh come on. Nobody likes two different kinds of eggs equally. You like one better than the other and I wanna know which."

—Joey

Ross's Chilaquiles

YIELD:
6 servings

PREP AND COOK TIME:
1 hour

For unmentionable reasons, Ross can't eat tacos. But you know what Ross can eat? Chilaquiles! Okay, fine. Do you really want to know why Ross can't eat tacos? Let's just say there might have been some tacos he once ate out of the back of a vendor's trunk and—should we change the subject? Yes? Great! Serve with Chick and the Duck Fat Black Beans (page 56).

SALSA VERDE:

1½ pounds fresh peeled tomatillos or one 28-ounce can tomatillos
4 jalapenos, stemmed and halved
2 large yellow onions, quartered
Juice of 4 limes
4 garlic cloves, peeled
½ cup cilantro, chopped
1 tablespoon agave syrup (optional)
Salt and pepper

CHILAQUILES:

2 to 4 tablespoons canola oil, plus more as needed
16 day-old soft corn tortillas, quartered
Salt and pepper
6 eggs (optional)
Butter (optional)
3 avocados, sliced
8 ounces cotija or feta cheese
1 red onion or Pickled Red Onion (page 15), diced small
One 8-ounce container crème fraîche
½ cup cilantro, measured then chopped
2 limes, cut into wedges

✗ TIP: If you are using canned tomatillos, add the tomatillos with their juices from the can and all fresh ingredients directly to a blender; blend to desired consistency. Season with salt and pepper to taste.

FOR THE SALSA VERDE:

In a large pot, add the tomatillos, jalapenos, onions, lime juice, and garlic, and fill the pot with water until the ingredients are just covered. Bring water to a boil, then reduce the heat to medium. Allow to cook uncovered for an additional 10 minutes, until the tomatillos slightly change color. Remove from the heat.

Add cilantro and the ingredients from the pot to a blender, and blend to the desired consistency. Blend until toothsome, but almost smooth, 2 to 3 minutes. Season with agave, salt, and pepper to taste.

FOR THE CHILAQUILES:

Coat the bottom of a large deep pan with the oil. Heat on medium-high.

Once the oil is hot, and working in batches, add the quartered tortillas (make sure that the tortillas are not sticking together; using a slotted spoon helps), and allow to crisp until almost golden, 1 to 2 minutes. Remove from the heat, and place in a ceramic dish or on a large plate lined with paper towels.

Add 2 teaspoons of oil to pan with 1½ cups of the salsa verde. Heat on medium until the salsa begins to bubble a little and thicken, 2 to 3 minutes.

Once the salsa verde is hot, toss in the fried tortillas. Coat the tortillas in the salsa, being careful to not break them. If needed, add a tablespoon of salsa at a time until the chips are fully coated. The tortillas should not be soggy, but they should be well coated with salsa. Season with salt and pepper to taste.

If you are using eggs, heat a large nonstick pan on medium-low. Add in a generous tablespoon of butter and evenly distribute around the pan. Once the butter is melted and a bit frothy in the pan, crack the eggs directly into the pan and fry until sunny side up, 1 to 3 minutes. Season with salt and pepper to taste.

To serve, plate an even amount of chilaquiles on each plate. Garnish with avocado slices, crumbled cheese, red onion, drizzles of crème fraîche, and cilantro. Add a fried egg on top, if using. Serve with lime wedges.

1950s Diner Special:
Gentlemen Prefer Breakfast Sausage *and* Gravy

When Monica loses her last $127 trying to play the stock market, she's forced to take a job at a 1950s-themed diner. Soon she finds herself wearing a hoop skirt, a wig, and flame-retardant boobs, and dancing to "YMCA" on the counters in between serving up Laverne and Curly Fries and other classic diner dishes like this breakfast sausage and gravy.

BISCUITS:
2 cups all-purpose flour
½ teaspoon salt
1 tablespoon baking powder
6 tablespoons (¾ stick) unsalted butter, frozen and cut into pea-size cubes
1 cup buttermilk

SAUSAGE AND GRAVY:
10 ounces breakfast sausage
½ teaspoon flour
2½ cups milk
Salt and pepper
6 eggs (optional)
Butter (optional)
Cilantro, for garnish

A NOTE FROM CHEF MONICA: *Roux* is a mixture of cooked flour and fat—in this case, sausage drippings—used to thicken soups and sauces, like gravy. The mixture will darken as it cooks, but be careful to keep stirring so the roux doesn't burn.

TO MAKE THE BISCUITS:
In a large bowl, combine the flour, salt, and baking powder. Toss in the butter cubes and coat evenly with the flour mixture. Then, using your thumb and forefinger, snap the butter pieces so that they are flat, but still coated with flour.

Pour the buttermilk into the flour and butter mixture and mix until ingredients incorporate, about 2 to 3 minutes.

Turn out the incorporated dough onto a floured, nonporous surface and gently fold onto itself until smooth. Try not to overwork the dough, as you don't want the butter to become soft.

Roll out the dough so it is 1-inch thick, and cut out biscuits with a 2- or 3-inch biscuit cutter or other implements such as upside-down glasses or mason jar rings. Re-roll the leftover dough to cut out additional biscuits.

Preheat the oven to 375°F and line a baking sheet with parchment paper.

Arrange the biscuits on the prepared baking sheet, and place the biscuits in the refrigerator for 10 to 15 minutes.

Remove from the refrigerator and bake the biscuits for 10 to 15 minutes, until the tops are golden and the biscuits rise.

TO MAKE THE SAUSAGE AND GRAVY:
Heat a large heavy-bottomed pan on high. Once hot, add the breakfast sausage. Using a wooden spoon, break the sausage apart in chunks and allow to brown, 5 to 7 minutes. Remove the sausage and set aside, leaving the oil drippings in the pan.

Reduce the heat to medium, add the flour, and stir into the pan drippings to create a roux. Cook the roux, stirring constantly, for 2 to 3 minutes, until aromatic.

Whisk the milk into the roux until the mixture thickens, making a béchamel, 2 to 5 minutes. Salt and heavily pepper to taste.

If serving with eggs, heat a second pan on medium. Once hot, add about a tablespoon of butter to evenly coat the pan and, working in batches, crack the eggs into the pan and fry sunny-side up, 1 to 3 minutes to desired doneness.

To serve, cut open the biscuits and ladle the sausage gravy on top. Top each serving with an egg, if using.

Appetizers and Snacks

Just for Joey Fries Board

SERVES:
6 as an entrée,
12 as an appetizer
(1 Joey Tribbiani)

PREP AND COOK TIME:
1 hour

When Phoebe sets Joey up with her friend Sarah, she's surprised when he tells her he doesn't plan to call her again. Why? She took some of his fries! And fries represent all food! Joey doesn't share food!! It's one of his core principles. This fries board is loaded with three different styles of fries, so it's a big meal for one person, but you don't have to share if you don't want to.

2 large sweet potatoes, cut into batonnets, or frozen store-bought sweet potato fries

4 russet potatoes, cut into curly fries using a spiralizer, or frozen store-bought curly fries

6 purple potatoes, cut into wedges

1 cup cornstarch or potato starch, divided

2 quarts (8 cups) vegetable or canola oil for frying

Salt and pepper

3 cloves garlic, minced

½ cup grated Parmesan cheese

¼ cup fresh parsley, roughly chopped

2 to 3 tablespoons Tajín seasoning

Ranch BBQ Sauce (page 11), for serving

Cumin Chili Ketchup (page 11), for serving

Sriracha mayonnaise, for serving

A NOTE FROM CHEF MONICA: *Batonnet*
is French for stick or baton, which accurately describes what these potato spears will look like (basically a classic french fry shape). Start by cutting off the ends of the sweet potatoes, then slicing off the sides until you have a rectangle. Then cut the rectangle into slabs, and the slabs into strips.

If making from scratch, cut the potatoes then place them in separate containers filled with water. If using frozen store-bought potatoes, cook the potatoes according to the package directions, then skip to serving instructions.

Twenty minutes before frying, pat the potatoes dry, and first toss the sweet potatoes in cornstarch or potato starch until well coated, then place on a baking sheet lined with parchment paper. Next toss the russet potatoes in starch and set aside on a different tray to keep them separate. Do the same with the purple potatoes.

Line a few baking trays with parchment paper or paper towels and set aside.

In a large heavy pot, heat the oil to 375°F. Working in batches, use a slotted spoon to place the sweet potatoes in the oil, and fry until they rise to the top, about 5 minutes.

Remove the potatoes and spread evenly on a prepared baking sheet, making sure the fries aren't overlapping. Repeat the frying process with the rest of the fries, being sure to keep each kind of potato separate. Once all the fries are cooked, place the baking sheets in the freezer for 30 minutes.

Preheat the oven to 250°F.

Return the oven to 375°F, and working again in batches, fry the potatoes again until crisp—crunchy on the outside and tender in the middle—7 to 10 minutes. Transfer the fries to an oven-safe platter or baking tray lined with paper towels and season with salt and pepper to taste. Place the platter or tray in the oven to keep warm.

When ready to serve, using a large bowl, toss the purple potatoes in the garlic, Parmesan, and parsley, and stack on a large platter. Toss the curly fries in Tajín, and stack in a large pile on the board. Stack the sweet potato fries in the same way. Place the sauces in small bowls or ramekins and stagger on the board.

Fried Stuff With Cheese

"What's my little chef got for me tonight?" an overweight Joey asks Monica in the alternate universe where they're a couple instead of Monica and Chandler. "Your favorite," she replies with a smile. "Fried stuff with cheese!"

FRIED PICKLES:
20 kosher dill pickle chips, drained
2 cups buttermilk
4 tablespoons mustard powder, divided
4 tablespoons garlic powder, divided
½ cup Old Bay Seasoning or prepared dry rub barbecue seasoning, divided
Hot sauce
1½ quarts (6 cups) canola oil for frying
2 cups all-purpose flour
1 cup cornstarch

PIMENTO CHEESE:
2 cups shredded cheddar cheese
½ cup sour cream
½ cup mayonnaise
2 tablespoons Worcestershire sauce
1 tablespoon garlic powder
1 tablespoon onion powder
½ cup pimento peppers, diced, with 2 tablespoons juice reserved
Salt and pepper

TO MAKE THE FRIED PICKLES:
Place the pickles into an airtight food container with a lid.

In a small bowl, mix together the buttermilk, 2 tablespoons of the mustard powder, 2 tablespoons of the garlic powder, ¼ cup of the Old Bay or barbecue seasoning, and hot sauce to taste. Pour over the pickles and stir. Allow the pickles to marinate, covered, for up to 4 hours in the refrigerator.

An hour before serving, remove the pickles from the refrigerator and allow to come to room temperature.

In a large or medium heavy pot, heat the oil to 375°F.

In a large bowl, mix together the flour, cornstarch, and remaining spices. Toss the pickles into the flour and make sure they are well coated.

Working in batches, use a slotted spoon to fry the pickles until they are golden on one side, about 2 minutes. Once golden, flip and fry the other side, 1 to 2 minutes longer. Transfer to a platter lined with paper towels. Do not overcrowd the pot, and be sure the oil returns to 375°F between batches.

TO MAKE THE PIMENTO CHEESE:
In a food processor, blend the cheddar cheese, sour cream, mayonnaise, Worcestershire sauce, garlic powder, onion powder, and pimento peppers until well incorporated, but still chunky, 2 to 3 minutes. Season with salt and pepper to taste, then serve in a small bowl alongside the fried pickles.

Wedding Pigs in a Blanket

When Monica is rushing to finish the food for Carol and Susan's wedding, Joey is put in charge of assembling the pigs in a blanket. A classic and delicious appetizer to serve at any event, these pigs won't be reluctant to get in the blankets and will surely wow your friends and family. Before you know it, you'll be bragging about how you wrapped those bad boys yourself!

One 8-ounce tube crescent rolls
One 5.2-ounce package Gournay cheese, such as Boursin
One 12-ounce package mini cocktail wieners

Preheat the oven to 375°F.

Unroll the crescent roll sheets and tear or cut along each perforated line. Cut each triangle into three smaller triangles.

Place a smear of cheese along the shortest edge of a crescent roll triangle.

Place one cocktail wiener on the cheese, then gently roll the dough and wiener together to the pointed side.

Transfer to a baking sheet and bake until golden, 12 to 15 minutes.

You Know What They Say About Oysters

YIELD:
6 servings

PREP AND COOK TIME:
30 minutes

When the gang imagines what their lives could have been, Monica's alternate reality is one where she's still a virgin at age thirty. Desperate to just get it over with and give someone her flower, she cooks oysters for her boyfriend to try to get him in the mood. You may want to serve these classic aphrodisiacs with a Middle Eastern couscous you can eat with your hands. That's sensual, right?

12 fresh oysters
½ cup Rapini Pesto, the Best-O
  (page 10) or store-bought pesto
½ cup Ham Spread (page 10)
½ cup grated Parmesan cheese
Fresh dill sprigs, for garnish

Preheat the oven's broiler and line a baking sheet with parchment paper.

Open the oysters on the half shell and place on the prepared baking sheet.

Scoop an even layer of pesto and ham spread into each oyster. Top with Parmesan.

Broil until the cheese is bubbly with speckles of brown spots, 2 to 3 minutes. Garnish with fresh dill, and serve immediately.

Crab Cakes

When Ross is stood up on a blind date, the waiters offer to show him a good time by bringing him a crab cake appetizer on the house. Ross later discovers that the waiters have a pool going on how long it will take him to realize he's being stood up and leave. Feeling insulted, Ross decides to leave immediately, but not without his free crab cakes!

1 large shallot
Olive oil, for drizzling
Salt and pepper
½ cup crème fraîche
1 pound jumbo lump crab meat
⅓ cup chopped chives
⅓ cup roughly chopped dill
1 tablespoon Worcestershire sauce
1 egg
1 tablespoon Old Bay Seasoning
¾ cup panko bread crumbs
Canola or vegetable oil for frying
Fried eggs (optional)
Sriracha mayonnaise
Pickled Greene Tomatoes (page 58)

Preheat the oven to 350°F and line a baking sheet with parchment paper.

Remove the skin from shallot, and crush the shallot using a rolling pin or the back of a knife. Drizzle with olive oil, and sprinkle with salt and pepper. Place on the prepared baking sheet. Bake the shallot until soft and aromatic, about 20 minutes.

Using a blender, blend together roasted shallot and crème fraîche. Set aside.

In a medium bowl, mix together the crab, chives, dill, Worcestershire sauce, egg, Old Bay Seasoning, bread crumbs, and salt and pepper to taste. Make sure all ingredients are well incorporated.

Place in an airtight container and allow to marinate in the refrigerator for 1 to 4 hours.

Line a baking sheet with parchment paper and form the crab mixture into 4-inch patties. Place patties on the baking sheet.

Heat a medium frying pan on high. Once hot, reduce heat to medium and add in oil until it comes up ½-inch high on the pan.

Working in batches, add the crab cakes to the pan and fry until crisp and golden brown, 2 minutes. Using a fish spatula, flip and crisp the other side, 2 to 3 minutes more. Place on a plate or platter lined with paper towels.

Serve with fried eggs, if using, the shallot crème fraîche, sriracha mayonnaise, and Pickled Greene Tomatoes.

Tag on a Cracker Tuna Dip

Season 7, Episode 5
"The One With the Engagement Picture"

YIELD: 6 servings
PREP AND COOK TIME: 1 hour

Rachel's attractive young assistant, Tag, has very little experience—three years painting houses, two whole summers working at a restaurant—but sometimes he does sit-ups in the office during lunch, which is certainly a skill. He's so good looking, she could eat him on a cracker! Not that she would *ever* act on her feelings. Nope, Rachel Greene is nothing if not professional.

Two 5-ounce cans albacore tuna in water, drained
4 ounces cream cheese
⅓ cup mayonnaise
1½ tablespoons Worcestershire sauce
Zest and juice of 1 lemon
1 teaspoon liquid smoke (optional)
1 teaspoon smoked paprika
¼ cup fresh chives, measured then chopped, plus more for garnish
¼ cup fresh dill, measured then chopped
½ tablespoon garlic powder
Salt and pepper
One 10-ounce package flatbread crackers, store-bought

In a food processor, combine the tuna, cream cheese, mayonnaise, Worcestershire sauce, lemon zest and juice, liquid smoke (if using), paprika, chives, dill, and garlic powder, and process until incorporated and smooth, 2 to 3 minutes. Season with salt and pepper to taste.

Scrape into a serving bowl and top with additional chives. Serve with flatbread crackers.

A NOTE FROM CHEF MONICA:
Use dolphin-safe tuna for this dish!

Shrimp Ceviche in Ponzu Sauce
With Fried Wonton Skins

YIELD:
6 servings

PREP AND COOK TIME:
40 minutes

Monica lands a job interview for the restaurant of her dreams. In an attempt to wow the owner, Steve, she meticulously prepares a shrimp ravioli in ponzu sauce with cilantro and just a touch of minced ginger for the first course. However, Steve gets high on the way to the interview and eats them in a flash, saying he could eat a hundred of them. If Monica had made this shrimp ceviche instead, she might have been able to make enough to slow him down until the next course was ready. The interview is a bust, but this dish is amazing. Serve with Monica's Onion Galette (page 95) eight and a half minutes later.

FRIED WONTON SKINS:
One 14-ounce package wonton or egg-roll skins
1½ quarts (6 cups) canola or vegtable oil for frying
Salt and pepper

CEVICHE:
1 teaspoon grated fresh ginger
½ cup ponzu sauce
¼ cup pineapple juice
1 garlic clove, minced
1 cup pineapple, small diced
1 medium red onion, diced
2 Fresno chiles, diced
2 pounds 16/20 raw shrimp, tails removed and cut into 1-inch pieces
1 cup cilantro, roughly chopped
Salt and pepper
Cilantro sprigs, for garnishing
Lime wedge, for garnish

TO MAKE THE FRIED WONTON SKINS:
Using a pizza slicer, cut the wonton or eggroll skins into 1½-inch-wide strips. Set on a baking sheet lined with parchment paper, and cover with a damp tea towel.

On medium high, heat the oil in a large heavy pot until it reaches 300°F.

Once hot, reduce the heat to medium, and working in batches, place the strips in the oil and fry until they have bubbly skin and are blonde, about 1 minute. Flip and fry on the other side, about 1 minute more.

Remove the strips using a slotted spoon and place on a large plate lined with paper towels. Season with salt and pepper to taste.

TO MAKE THE CEVICHE:
In a blender, combine the ginger, ponzu sauce, pineapple juice, and garlic, and process until incorporated, 2 to 3 minutes.

In a large bowl, combine the pineapple, onion, chiles, and shrimp. Pour in the ponzu marinade, toss to combine, and allow the shrimp to cure for 15 to 20 minutes. The shrimp will begin to go from gray to a light translucent pink, "cooking" in the sauce.

Before serving, toss in the cilantro. Season with salt and pepper to taste, then serve, stacking the ceviche high in a bowl, and top with a few sprigs of cilantro and a lime wedge for garnish. Serve with fried wonton skins.

Janice's Artichoke Dip

Classic artichoke dip is a hit at any party. When Monica serves it on New Year's Eve, Janice can't get enough of it. "The diet starts tomorrow!" she declares.

1 cup grated Parmesan cheese, divided
⅓ cup crème fraîche
One 8-ounce can artichoke hearts, drained
Zest and juice of 1 lemon
2 garlic cloves, finely grated
Salt and pepper
Emergency Garlic Bread (opposite) or crackers, for serving

Preheat the oven to 350°F.

In a food processor, add ¾ cup of the Parmesan, the crème fraîche, artichoke hearts, lemon zest and juice, and garlic cloves, and process until incorporated, 2 to 3 minutes. Season to taste with salt and pepper, and process again to combine. Transfer to a baking dish and bake until golden brown, 15 to 20 minutes.

Heat a medium nonstick pan on medium. Once hot, place 1 to 2 tablespoons of the remaining Parmesan in the pan in a pile, and allow to melt and crisp to form a chip, about 3 to 5 minutes. Remove from heat and place on a baking sheet lined with parchment paper. Repeat with the remaining Parmesan.

To serve, place artichoke dip in a bowl, place a Parmesan chip or two in the center of the dip, so that they are upright, and serve with Emergency Garlic Bread or crackers.

Emergency Garlic Bread

Can you believe Chandler and Monica don't trust Joey or Phoebe with keys to their apartment after all these years? Neither can they. When Chandler and Monica leave on their honeymoon, and Joey and Phoebe realize they have stuff they absolutely need in there—a guitar and chicken Parm, obviously—so they call their building superintendent, Treeger, and say it's an emergency gas leak. Oh, and to bring garlic bread.

1 round, crusty sourdough loaf
5 to 6 garlic cloves, minced
1 cup (2 sticks) unsalted butter, at room temperature
⅓ cup grated Parmesan cheese (optional)
¼ cup parsley, minced
Salt and pepper

Preheat the oven to 350°F and line a baking sheet with parchment paper.

Cut the sourdough loaf into 2-inch thick slices, and place face up on the prepared baking sheet.

In a small bowl, stir together the garlic, butter, Parmesan if using, and parsley.

Using a food safe brush or a rubber spatula, spread the butter mixture over each slice of bread.

Toast in the oven, until the bread is crispy and golden, about 10 minutes. Sprinkle with salt and pepper to taste, then serve hot.

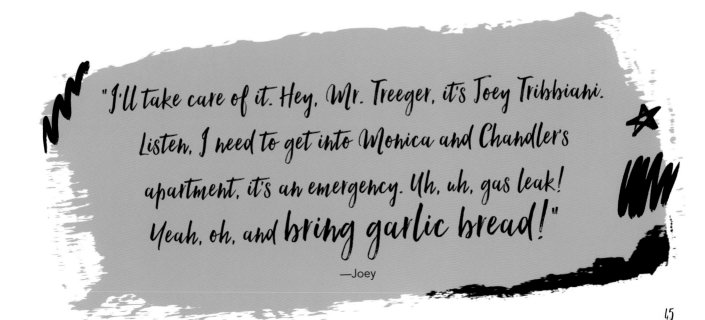

"I'll take care of it. Hey, Mr. Treeger, it's Joey Tribbiani. Listen, I need to get into Monica and Chandler's apartment, it's an emergency. Uh, uh, gas leak! Yeah, oh, and bring garlic bread!"

—Joey

Milk That You Chew:
Tips for Assembling the Perfect Cheese Plate

Everyone always looks to Chandler to be the witty, funny, and sarcastic one of the group—maybe this statistical analyst with an affinity for data reconfiguration really does have a better shot at pursuing a job in advertising. Check out his creative sales pitch for cheese, and try to assemble a spread.

STEP 1: MILK THAT YOU CHEW
You don't have to leave cheese plates to the professionals! When assembling a delicious cheese plate or board, try to think about using different cheeses from different milk types: cow, goat, and sheep. Also think about varying the textures of cheeses. Start off by picking three cheese textures from different milk types: try a hard, aged cheese like aged goat Gouda; a semisoft sheep cheese like petit Basque; and a soft cow cheese like Brie. To plate, cut aged Gouda in rectangular slices and petit Basque in wedges, and stagger these on a large board or serving platter. Leave the Brie whole, and place in the middle of the plate or board. Some cheeses have rinds that aren't suitable for eating, so be sure to remove those before serving.

STEP 2: CRACKERS—BECAUSE YOUR CHEESE NEEDS A BUDDY
Chandler is right, your cheese does need a buddy, but the buddy doesn't always have to come in the form of a cracker. Other buddies can include various cured meats and charcuterie, breadsticks, baked breads, and nuts. When pairing your cheese with a buddy, think about the cheese's tasting notes. Is it mildly sweet and buttery like petit Basque? Maybe try pairing it with cured meats, and salted or candied almonds. Is it creamy and milder with hints of mushrooms, like Brie?

Serve with warm baguette slices. To plate, place the buddies next to their complementary cheeses, piling high on the platter, but be careful not to overload. If you're using almonds or a different type of nut, consider putting them in a small ceramic or glass bowl before placing on the plate or board.

STEP 3: A GRAPE—BECAUSE WHO CAN GET A WATERMELON IN YOUR MOUTH?

Fruit is an excellent accompaniment for most cheeses. Honeycrisp apple slices pair wonderfully with aged Gouda, and green grapes go so nicely with petit Basque. But you don't have to limit yourself to fresh fruits. Try fig jam with petit Basque or Brie, or mustard with aged Gouda and apples. Just be sure to sprinkle a little bit of lemon juice over your apples to prevent them from browning. To finish plating, take scissors or cooking shears and cut small clusters of grapes so that guests can pick up five or six at a time without having to wrestle them off their vines. Place the clusters in the empty spaces on your cheese plate or board. Next, take your apple slices, and place them with a small ramekin of mustard next to your aged Gouda. Quarter a few black mission figs for garnish, and place them on top of the Brie. Fill a small ramekin with fig jam, and place next to the Brie or petit Basque.

Sides

Mmm . . . Noodle Soup!

Cold Cucumber and Peach Soup

Rachel's Side Salad

Melanie's Fruit Salad

Magic Beans

Chick and the Duck Fat Black Beans

Kale Slaw

Pickled Greene Tomatoes

Cherry Couscous With Brown Butter

Mmm . . . Noodle Soup!

YIELD:
6 servings

PREP AND COOK TIME:
1½ hours

When Joey auditions for a commercial where he's a dad eating soup with his kid, he can't quite get his lines right. "Mmm, soup," is all he has to say. But he just can't stop saying, "Mmm, noodle soup!" Whatever line you say, this soup is sure to warm the bones. The egg brings a hearty and yet airy thickness to the soup without causing it to have the consistency of a stew.

8 cups Turkey Stock (page 14)

4 eggs, separated

Zest and juice of 2 small lemons, divided

1 pound chicken sausage, cut into 2-inch pieces

8 ounces alphabet pasta

1 tablespoon crushed red pepper flakes

1 cup chiffonade-cut kale (page 57)

Salt and pepper

In a large stock pot, heat the turkey stock on medium-high until it comes to a rolling boil, then reduce the heat to medium.

In a large bowl, use a hand mixer on medium-high speed to beat the egg whites until they form soft peaks, 2 to 3 minutes. While you are beating the eggs, add the juice of one lemon.

In a medium bowl, whisk the egg yolks until pale in color, and gently fold into the egg whites. Slowly ladle in a bit of the turkey broth to temper the eggs.

Once tempered, gently add the egg mixture back into the broth, stirring constantly to prevent the egg from curdling. Stir until the broth thickens, about 5 minutes.

Once broth thickens, add the sausage. Allow the sausage to cook for 4 to 5 minutes, then add the pasta. Allow to cook for 5 to 7 minutes, until the pasta is al dente and has grown in size. Remove the pot from the heat, add the crushed red pepper flakes and kale, stir, and cover.

Allow the soup to sit covered for about 5 minutes, until the kale softens. Season with additional lemon juice, salt, and pepper to taste.

A NOTE FROM CHEF MONICA:
To temper, a hot liquid is gradually added to eggs in small amounts and slowly to prevent curdling.

Cold Cucumber and Peach Soup

Season 2, Episode 5
"The One With Five
Steaks and an Eggplant"

YIELD: 6 servings
PREP TIME: 30 minutes
INACTIVE TIME: 2 to 6 hours

When the gang is out for dinner to celebrate Monica's promotion, not everyone can afford an expensive dish. But that doesn't mean that Phoebe's low-price cup of cold cucumber soup has to be boring. This version includes peaches, yogurt, and fresh mint, and is a cinch to whip up in a blender.

1½ cups goat milk yogurt or
  Greek yogurt
1 large cucumber, diced
4 to 6 medium peaches, peeled
  and diced
2 tablespoons honey
1 tablespoon Modena white vinegar
  or white wine vinegar
½ cup water
8 to 10 mint leaves
Freshly ground black pepper

In a blender, combine all ingredients but the mint and pepper. Blend on high speed until smooth, 1 to 2 minutes. Place in an airtight container and refrigerate for 2 to 6 hours.

Once cold and ready to serve, place in bowls and garnish with mint sprigs and freshly ground black pepper.

Rachel's Side Salad

Season 2, Episode 5
"The One With Five
Steaks and an Eggplant"

YIELD: 2 servings
PREP TIME: 20 minutes

Even if money is a little tight, this salad can be more than an accompaniment to your water!

2 baby radishes, washed and thinly sliced

3 or 4 garlic scapes, washed, or 2 garlic cloves

¼ cup extra-virgin olive oil, plus more for drizzling

Salt and pepper

4 teaspoons champagne vinegar

½ blood orange or standard orange, juiced

1½ tablespoons honey

2 heads little gems lettuce or 1 head romaine lettuce, halved

Place thinly sliced radish in a small bowl and cover with cold water to prevent discoloring. Set aside.

Preheat the oven to 425°F and line a baking sheet with foil.

Place the garlic scapes on the prepared baking sheet, drizzle with olive oil, and sprinkle with salt. If using regular garlic skip to next step. Roast scapes in the oven until soft, 7 to 10 minutes. Remove and set aside.

In a food processor, add the roasted scapes or garlic, champagne vinegar, orange juice, and honey, and pulse until vinaigrette begins to form. While pulsing, slowly add in the olive oil until the mixture thickens, 3 to 5 minutes. Season with salt and pepper to taste.

Drain the radishes and pat dry.

To assemble the salad, stagger the halved little gems on a plate and sprinkle 3 to 5 radish slices over each gem half. Finish by generously drizzling with the dressing.

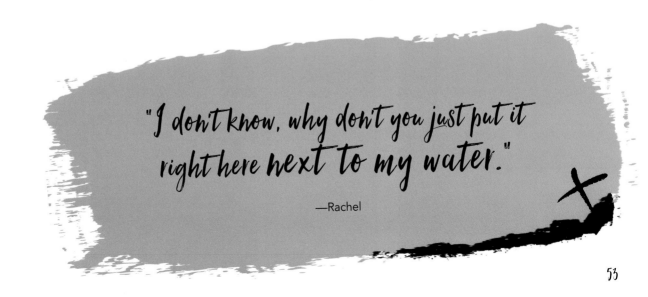

"I don't know, why don't you just put it right here next to my water."

—Rachel

Melanie's Fruit Salad

When Joey's broke, he participates in a sperm study to make some extra cash and is prohibited from conducting any, ahem, personal experiments. His girlfriend at the time, Melanie, grows quite attached after he does things to her in bed that he doesn't normally do. Since Melanie's job is making fruit baskets, she makes sure Joey has an endless supply to show her thanks.

¼ cup sugar
½ cup white vinegar
1 large pineapple, peeled and cut into 2-inch chunks
2 large grapefruits, supremed
½ cup mint leaves, torn
Aleppo chile flakes or crushed red pepper flakes
Salt and pepper (optional)
Extra-virgin olive oil (optional)

Heat a medium saucepan on medium-low, and add the sugar and vinegar.

Stirring occasionally, allow the sugar and vinegar mixture to thicken until the mixture resembles a loose syrup and can coat the back of a wooden spoon, 5 to 7 minutes. Once thickened, remove from the heat and set aside.

Stagger pineapple and grapefruit segments on a large serving plate, and drizzle with the reduced vinegar mixture.

Evenly sprinkle the torn mint and Aleppo chile flakes on top.

For a more savory fruit salad, season with salt and pepper to taste, and consider adding just a drizzle of olive oil.

A NOTE FROM CHEF MONICA:
"Supreme" is a fancy word for segmenting citrus and removing the membrane between each piece. Peel the fruit with a sharp knife, then make careful cuts in between the flesh of each segment and the membrane.

Magic Beans

Welcome to the real world, Rachel! After Rachel leaves Barry at the altar and moves in with Monica, she cuts up Daddy's credit cards, some guy named FICA takes all her money, and she finds herself getting coffee (and it's not even for her!). Though she doesn't feel okay, Phoebe and Monica reassure her that she's being amazing and independent, and even though she gave up an orthodontist, she's got some magic beans and a beanstalk full of possibilities. But even if all she's got are beans, Rachel could turn them into this magical beans recipe and be just fine, with a little help from her friends.

2 strips thick-sliced applewood bacon, diced
1 small yellow onion, diced
Salt and pepper
One 28-ounce can of pork and beans
¼ cup molasses
¼ cup packed brown sugar
¼ cup ketchup
2 teaspoons mustard powder
2 tablespoons apple cider vinegar

Heat a large nonstick skillet on medium-high. Once hot, reduce the heat to medium and add the diced bacon. Cook until crispy and firm, 7 to 8 minutes.

Using a slotted spoon, remove the bacon from the pan and place on a plate lined with paper towels. Next, add the onion and sauté in the bacon drippings until browned, 5 to 7 minutes. Season with pepper.

Place the pork and beans in a medium pot on low heat. Add the bacon bits and onion, and stir.

Add the molasses, brown sugar, ketchup, mustard powder, and apple cider vinegar to the pot. Stir until well incorporated. Allow beans to simmer, 5 to 10 minutes. Season with salt and pepper to taste.

A NOTE FROM CHEF MONICA:
If you're still working on making the rest of your meal, these beans can be left on super low until you're ready to serve. Just stir them occasionally! Pair with Bathtub Fried Chicken (page 105) for a delicious meal.

Chick and the Duck Fat Black Beans

YIELD: 6 servings
PREP AND COOK TIME: 1 hour

Chandler and Joey are unlikely parents to a chick and a duck, but the four of them make a sweet little family. When the chick "goes through some changes" it grows into a rooster that wakes Rachel at dawn. She would probably enjoy the chick more if he were served with some black beans and maybe Ross's Chilaquiles (page 29).

These are also great with Ross's Hand-Scalding Fajitas (page 107). If eating with Ross's Chilaquiles, pair with a delicious mimosa and Melanie's Fruit Salad (page 54).

One 15-ounce can black beans
¾ cup Vegetable Stock (page 14)
2 tablespoons dried oregano
Juice of 1 orange
2 to 4 garlic cloves, minced
½ cup duck fat or coconut oil
Salt and pepper

In a medium pot, combine the black beans with the liquid, vegetable stock, oregano, orange juice, and garlic. Heat on medium until simmering, 5 to 7 minutes.

Reserve ¼ cup of the bean liquid from the pot and strain the rest.

Heat a large pan on medium high. Once hot, add the duck fat or coconut oil and beans. Allow beans to come to almost a rolling boil in the duck fat. Begin to mash. If the beans begin to dry out, reduce the heat and spoon in reserved liquid. Continue to mash until the beans have bite to them but are smooth, 3 to 5 minutes. Season with salt and pepper to taste.

Kale Slaw

Serve the salad with a nice dry Riesling, complete with candles and The One With the Large Candy Bar Pie (page 158) for dessert.

1 large shallot

1 teaspoon olive oil, plus more for dressing and kale

Salt and pepper

One 8-ounce container crème fraîche or low-fat Greek yogurt

¼ cup tahini

Juice of ½ lemon

1 large bunch kale (12 to 16 stems), stemmed

1 carrot, shredded

½ cup smoked almonds, measured and roughly chopped

Preheat the oven to 300°F and line a baking sheet with parchment paper.

Peel the shallot, drizzle with olive oil, and sprinkle with salt and pepper. Place the shallot on the prepared baking sheet and bake until soft and aromatic, 10 to 15 minutes. Set aside.

Place the crème fraîche or Greek yogurt, tahini, and lemon juice in a blender, and pulse to combine. Add the shallot and blend on medium-high speed until a dressing forms, about 1 minute. If the dressing is too watery, you can drizzle in a small amount of olive oil while you blend. If dressing is too thick, you can add in more lemon juice as you blend. Season with salt and pepper to taste. The dressing can be made the day before serving and refrigerated overnight. Allow to rest at room temperature for 15 minutes before assembling the salad.

While the dressing is resting, massage the kale leaves for a few minutes with some olive oil to tenderize. Prepare chiffonade by stacking the leaves, then rolling them tightly lengthwise, and use a sharp knife to slice into thin ribbons. Mix the kale with shredded carrots, toss with the dressing, and pile high in a bowl and top generously with smoked almonds.

Pickled Greene Tomatoes

Season 2, Episode 7
"The One Where Ross Finds Out"

YIELD: 6 servings
PREP AND COOK TIME: 40 minutes

The *Friends* gang aren't big drinkers, but every now and then even they can't help but drown their sorrows. Just when Rachel realizes her feelings for Ross, he starts dating Julie! In response, Rachel has a few too many drinks and gets so pickled she borrows a cellphone from a stranger to tell Ross she's over him. Which she definitely, totally is. And that, my friend, is what they call closure.

Enjoy with The One With the Picnic Basket (Duck Rillettes) (page 108) and baguettes or crackers, or at Ugly Naked Guy's Sausage Party (page 98).

6 to 8 small to medium green
  tomatoes, cut into wedges
½ lemon, peeled and cut into
  segments
3 or 4 garlic cloves
3 tablespoons pink peppercorns
½ cup sugar
½ teaspoon kosher salt
1½ cups apple cider vinegar
½ cup water
1 tablespoon culinary lavender
  (optional)
¼ cup bourbon

Place tomato slices in a sterile 1-liter pickling jar. Add the lemon, garlic cloves, and peppercorns to the jar.

In a medium pot, combine the sugar, salt, apple cider vinegar, water, lavender, and bourbon. Heat on medium until the ingredients come to a simmer or until the salt and sugar have incorporated into the liquid, 10 to 12 minutes.

Add the liquid to pickling jar. Cover the jar with a clean tea towel or cheesecloth, until liquid is cool. Once cool, top with the lid and refrigerate for at least 4 hours.

Cherry Couscous
With Brown Butter

Season 6,
Episodes 15 AND 16
"The One That Could Have
Been, Parts 1 and 2"

YIELD: 6 servings
PREP AND COOK TIME: 25 minutes

In an alternate reality, Monica is a thirty-year-old dating Dr. Roger, a know-it-all whom she likes enough to consider "giving him her flower." She makes him a romantic dinner, including couscous, which is abandoned when he's called to the hospital. When Chandler—Monica's real soul mate—shows up to dine with her instead, he tries to make her feel better by imitating Dr. Roger so it's like he's there. Did you know they didn't add the second "cous" until 1979?

To make your own romantic dinner, serve with You Know What They Say About Oysters (page 39). If you're bringing this dish on a picnic to serve with The One With the Picnic Basket (Duck Rillettes) (page 108), it can be stored in an airtight container and is delicious cold the next day.

1¾ cups Vegetable Stock (page 14) or store-bought stock
¼ cup dried cherries
1 cup couscous
½ cup (1 stick) salted butter
Salt and pepper
10 to 12 sprigs fresh mint, torn
Zest of ½ lemon
1 teaspoon ground cinnamon
1 teaspoon ground cardamom
¼ cup roasted almond slivers

In a medium pot, combine the vegetable stock and cherries, and heat on medium-high until it reaches a rolling boil. Once boiling, turn off the heat and stir in the couscous. Remove the pot from heat completely, cover, and allow to sit until couscous has absorbed all of the water and has softened, 5 to 10 minutes. If the couscous is still a bit crunchy after 10 minutes, allow it to sit for a few additional minutes.

In a small pot, heat the butter on medium. Allow butter to melt and start to turn brown, about 5 minutes. Keep an eye on the butter, as it can go from melted to burnt quickly. It should start to smell nutty and have a brown but clear color to it. Remove from the heat.

Transfer the couscous to a large bowl, and gently break up clumps by gently tossing it with a fork. Slowly add in drizzles of the brown butter to taste. The couscous should taste nice and rich, but you don't want it to be greasy. Season with salt and pepper to taste.

Evenly sprinkle in the mint, lemon zest, cinnamon, cardamom, and roasted almond slivers. Give the whole dish a toss, and enjoy!

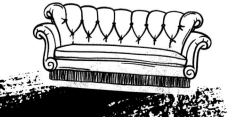

Sandwiches

The Moist Maker

Monica's Meatloaf Sandwich

Ross's Threesome Turkey Pastrami Sandwich

Spaghetti Sandwich

Rachel's Lobster With a Side of Lobster Roll

Joey's Meatball Sub

Olive Loaf and Ham Spread Sandwich

Open-Face How You Doin'? Chicken Salad Sandwich

No Five Steaks, Just an Eggplant Wrap

Did I Buy a Falafel From You Yesterday?

Chandler's Grilled Cheese

The Moist Maker

According to Ross, Monica makes the best leftover turkey sandwiches. The key is an extra slice of gravy-soaked bread in the middle: the moist maker. Try not to get angry if your boss eats most of your delicious sandwich without asking. Try even harder to keep your cool when you find out he threw some of it away—even if you're thirty years old, twice divorced, just got evicted, and that sandwich was the only good thing going on in your life.

3 slices sandwich bread
Mayonnaise (optional)
2 pieces romaine lettuce
½ cup leftover Turkey (page 129) or deli-style turkey slices
¼ cup leftover Cornbread Stuffing (page 131)
¼ cup leftover Gravy (page 130) or store-bought gravy
¼ cup Chandberry Sauce (page 131) or canned cranberry sauce
Salt and pepper

Lay out a slice of bread. If using mayonnaise, spread an even layer over the slice of bread then top with a leaf or two of lettuce, then half of the turkey, followed by half of the stuffing.

Pour the leftover gravy into a shallow dish. Dip a second slice of bread into the gravy and turn to coat. Top the stuffing with this moist maker slice.

Add another layer of lettuce, the remaining turkey, Chandberry Sauce, and top with the rest of the stuffing and the final slice of bread. Use a large toothpick to hold everything together.

"That sandwich was the **only good thing** going on in my life!"

—Ross

Monica's Meatloaf Sandwich

YIELD: 6 sandwiches
PREP AND COOK TIME: 1½ hours
INACTIVE TIME: 6 to 8 hours

Monica can make a wonderful meal out of anything! For Rachel's going away party, she once made smoked oyster casserole with a breakfast cereal crust, kidney beans in their own juices, and for dessert, a questionable orange. If none of those offerings tickle your fancy, try her meatloaf sandwich using leftover Tomato Jam (page 74) and Pimento Cheese (page 36).

MEATLOAF:
1½ pounds ground turkey
½ cup bread crumbs
1 medium white onion, diced
¼ cup milk
2 eggs
2 tablespoons thyme, roughly chopped
2 tablespoons oregano, roughly chopped
1 tablespoon mustard powder
1 tablespoon garlic salt
1½ tablespoons Worcestershire sauce
½ teaspoon pepper
Cooking spray
Apricot jam

SANDWICH:
Mayonnaise
Mustard
12 slices Texas toast, lightly toasted
Pimento Cheese (page 36) or store-bought
Tomato Jam (page 74) or store-bought
12 slices bacon, cooked
1 head romaine lettuce

TO MAKE THE MEATLOAF:
Preheat the oven to 375°F.

In a large bowl, use your hands to mix all the meatloaf ingredients except the cooking spray and jam until well incorporated. Be careful not to overmix, as this will make the ground turkey tough.

Evenly spray a 8½-by-4½-by-2½-inch loaf pan with cooking spray and place meat mixture inside. Top generously with apricot jam, and bake for about 45 minutes, or until it reaches an internal temperature of 165°F.

Allow to cool at room temperature, then refrigerate overnight.

TO MAKE THE SANDWICH:
Smear an even layer of mayonnaise and mustard on one side of the toast. Smear an even layer of pimento cheese on the other piece of toast. Next, cut a thick slice of meatloaf and place it on the toast with the pimento cheese. Top with an even layer of tomato jam, 1 or 2 slices of bacon, and 1 or 2 leaves of lettuce. Top the sandwich with the other slice of toast. Repeat with the remaining ingredients.

Ross's Threesome Turkey Pastrami Sandwich

Season 6, Episode 16
"The One That Could Have Been, Part 2"

YIELD: 3 sandwiches
PREP AND COOK TIME: 30 minutes

What if Carol hadn't realized she was a lesbian? That's the question Ross asks of an alternate reality in which he and Carol hadn't divorced. To spice up their sex life, they decide to have a threesome and invite a woman named Susan from Carol's gym to participate. The result? Ross ends up feeling a little bored and a bit left out, but on the upside, he makes a great turkey sandwich while he kills time. Ross's turkey sandwich just has a little mustard, but this pastrami with Russian dressing would also be a good consolation for a threesome-turned-twosome.

RUSSIAN DRESSING:
½ small yellow onion, chopped
2 tablespoons horseradish
¼ cup ketchup
½ cup mayonnaise
1 teaspoon sweet paprika
2 or 3 dashes hot sauce
1 tablespoon Worcestershire sauce

SANDWICH:
½ pound turkey pastrami
3 slices Swiss cheese
6 slices pumpernickel bread
1 cup Kale Slaw (page 57)

TO MAKE THE RUSSIAN DRESSING:
In a food processor, combine all the ingredients and blend until smooth, 2 to 3 minutes. Refrigerate for up to 1 week.

TO MAKE THE SANDWICH:
Heat a medium nonstick pan on medium. Once hot, pile together 3 or 4 slices of turkey pastrami per sandwich. Place a slice of Swiss cheese over the pastrami piles and sprinkle 2 or 3 tablespoons of water around pastrami and cheese. Cover the pan with a lid or a plate. Allow the cheese to melt, about 2 minutes. Uncover and remove from the pan.

To assemble the sandwich, smear Russian dressing on two pieces of bread. Top one slice of bread with kale slaw and a pastrami and swiss stack. Top with the other slice of bread. Repeat with the remaining ingredients to assemble additional sandwiches.

Spaghetti Sandwich

Like pizza, spaghetti is a staple in the *Friends* universe. When Rachel moves in with Joey after Phoebe's apartment catches fire, Rachel discovers living at Joey's is fun, and they eat big plates of spaghetti, while purposely dropping some on the floor. In celebration of all things spaghetti, I offer you the spaghetti sandwich! This works very well with leftover spaghetti, if you have it on hand.

2 tablespoons olive oil
¼ pound ground beef or turkey
1 cup Joey's Marinara Sauce (page 79)
6 ounces spaghetti noodles, cooked according to the package instructions
2 garlic cloves, finely minced
2 tablespoons unsalted butter, softened
2 tablespoons parsley, minced
Salt and pepper
4 slices Texas toast or thick-cut white bread
⅓ cup shredded mozzarella cheese

Heat a large pan on high. Once the pan is hot, reduce the heat to medium and add the oil. Allow the oil to heat for 1 minute. Add ground beef or turkey, stirring occasionally, and cook until brown, 3 to 4 minutes.

Add the marinara sauce and cooked spaghetti, tossing to make sure that pasta is well coated with sauce. Once the pasta is coated, remove from the heat and set aside.

In a small bowl, mix together the garlic, butter, parsley, salt and pepper to taste.

Using a rubber spatula, coat one side of each slice of bread with the butter mixture.

Heat a medium pan on high. Once hot, reduce the heat to medium and place two bread slices butter-side down in the pan. Top the bread with a generous scoop of spaghetti, mozzarella cheese, and a second slice of buttered bread with the butter facing up. Allow the sandwich to toast and crisp on the first side, 3 to 5 minutes.

Once crisp, flip to the second side and allow bread to crisp and cheese to melt, 3 to 5 minutes more. Cut into squares or triangles and enjoy!

Rachel's Lobster With a Side of Lobster Roll

Season 2, Episode 14
"The One With the Prom Video"

YIELD: 6 sandwiches
PREP AND COOK TIME: 40 minutes

One could argue that Ross and Rachel are twin flames. Their on-and-off relationship is a constant throughout the series. Leave it to Phoebe to be the psychic and predict the inevitable. When an '80s home video surfaces of Rachel being stood up by her prom date and she realizes that Ross stepped in to take her, Rachel realizes their deep feelings for each other and kisses him. "See!" Phoebe chimes in, "He's your lobster!"

3 pounds large lobster claws,
  thawed if frozen
Zest and juice of 1 small lemon
½ cup mayonnaise
2 tablespoons diced fresh tarragon
½ cup chives, minced and divided,
  plus more for serving
2 tablespoons Old Bay Seasoning or
  dry rub seasoning for seafood
Salt and pepper
Sweet Hawaiian rolls or brioche
  hot dog buns
Butter

Heat a large pot of water on high. Once boiling, add the lobster claws. Boil until bright red, about 12 minutes.

While the claws are boiling, create an ice bath by adding water and ice to a large bowl. Remove the claws from the water when cooked and immediately place claws in the ice bath. Let sit for 5 to 10 minutes until cool, then crack the knuckles and remove the claw meat.

In a large bowl, mix together the claw meat, lemon juice and zest, mayonnaise, tarragon, chives, and seasoning. Season with salt and pepper to taste.

Place a large pan over medium-high heat. Split the Hawaiian rolls or hot dog buns and butter the insides, then flatten. Place a flattened roll butter-side down in the pan and lightly toast, about 1 minute.

To serve, scoop the lobster mixture into the roll and top with additional fresh chives.

Joey's Meatball Sub

YIELD:
6 sandwiches

PREP AND COOK TIME:
1½ hours

When Joey, Ross, and Chandler go on a ride-along with Phoebe's boyfriend the cop, his patrol car backfires. Scared and thinking they're being shot at, Joey jumps to cover Ross. Chandler gets upset and jealous, only to find out that Joey was trying to save his meatball sub, instead. It sounds crazy, but Joey's meatball sub is the greatest sandwich in the world. Be careful not to over-smell all of the mouthwatering goodness, or you'll suck up all the taste units.

MEATBALLS:
¾ pound ground pork
¾ pound ground beef
½ yellow onion, finely chopped
2 tablespoons oregano, measured and roughly chopped
2 tablespoons parsley, measured and roughly chopped
2 tablespoons thyme, measured and roughly chopped
2 tablespoons basil, measured and roughly torn
½ cup bread crumbs
⅓ cup red wine
2 eggs
⅓ cup pine nuts, toasted

SANDWICHES:
3 cups Joey's Marinara Sauce (page 79) or store-bought
Six 6-inch Italian sub rolls
12 slices mozzarella cheese
¼ cup grated Parmesan cheese
Fresh parsley, roughly chopped, for garnishing

TO MAKE THE MEATBALLS:
Preheat the oven to 375°F and line a baking sheet with parchment paper.

In a large bowl, use your hands to combine all the ingredients. Be careful not to overmix, as this will make the mixture tough.

Form meatballs 2 to 3 inches in diameter. Place the meatballs on the prepared baking sheet and bake until golden brown, about 20 minutes.

TO MAKE THE SANDWICHES:
In a large pot over medium heat, heat the marinara sauce. Once the meatballs are baked, place them in the marinara sauce and allow to simmer for 10 to 15 minutes.

While meatballs are simmering, cut the Italian subs three-quarters of the way open. Place 1 or 2 slices of cheese inside and place the Italian subs on a baking sheet. Bake in the oven until the cheese is soft and melted, about 5 minutes.

Once the subs are ready, place 3 or 4 meatballs inside each sub, being sure to include some of the sauce. Sprinkle with Parmesan cheese and parsley to serve.

Olive Loaf and Ham Spread Sandwich

Season 2, Episode 21
"The One With the Bullies"

YIELD: 1 sandwich
PREP AND COOK TIME: 1 hour

Phoebe's family tree is anything but straightforward, so when she finally musters the courage to visit her long-lost father upstate, she asks Rachel and Joey to come along. They oblige, but in natural Joey fashion, he brings a friend for the cab ride. Spoiler alert: The friend is food. A sandwich to be exact, one he calls "olive loaf and ham spread," but don't worry, there's no mayo on it—that would make it gross.

1 crusty baguette or two slices olive bread
2 tablespoons prepared olive tapenade
⅓ cup shredded Manchego or another white cheese of choice
⅓ cup Ham Spread (page 10)

Preheat the oven to 350°F.

Cut the baguette open three-quarters of the way through or lay the two slices of bread side-by-side. On one side, spread tapenade, and on the other side spread the Ham Spread.

Top either side with Manchego cheese and toast in the oven until the cheese is melted, 5 to 7 minutes, then fold and serve.

"Okay, go get the sandwich, get the sandwich, doggie. Good doggie, get the sandwich, get the-okay, Joey, the dog will lick himself but he will not touch your sandwich, what does that tell you?"

—Rachel

"Well if he's not going to eat it, I will."

—Joey

Open-Face How You Doin'? Chicken Salad Sandwich

Season 2, Episode 14
"The One With the Prom Video"

YIELD: 6 sandwiches
PREP TIME: 40 minutes
INACTIVE TIME: 2 to 3 hours

Joey can make anything sound sexy and dirty. It's his party trick.
Try saying "Grandma's chicken salad" in your sultriest voice.

Meat of ½ small roasted chicken, shredded
3 stalks celery, small diced
¼ cup fresh dill, measured and roughly chopped
¼ cup fresh tarragon, measured and roughly chopped (optional)
2 medium red apples, cored and small diced
Zest and juice of 1 large lemon
1 cup mayonnaise
Salt and pepper
6 slices rye bread
Pea shoots, for garnish (optional)

In a large bowl, mix together the chicken, celery, dill, tarragon, apple, lemon zest and juice, and mayonnaise until well incorporated, 2 to 3 minutes. Season with salt and pepper to taste. Place in an airtight container and refrigerate for at least 2 to 3 hours.

To serve, place a generous scoop of chicken salad on a slice of rye bread. Top with pea shoots. Repeat with the remaining ingredients.

No Five Steaks, Just an Eggplant Wrap

Season 2, Episode 5
"The One With Five Steaks and an Eggplant"

YIELD: 2 to 4 wraps
PREP AND COOK TIME: 30 minutes

When Monica and Chandler invite everyone out to an expensive birthday celebration for Ross, Rachel, Joey, and Phoebe become upset as they're tired of always doing expensive outings with the group despite their tighter budgets. As a remedy, Monica offers to cook a fancy dinner for six with five steaks and an eggplant for Phoebe. However, Joey, Phoebe, and Rachel refuse the dinner—and free concert tickets—thinking that the others are offering charity. If you'd like to spend time with your friends, but maybe not break the bank, try making them these eggplant wraps, no steaks included.

SPICY YOGURT:
½ cup Greek yogurt
1 tablespoon chili flakes
½ lemon, juiced
Salt and pepper

WRAPS:
3 tablespoons olive oil
½ tablespoon cumin seeds
1 large eggplant, cut into 2-inch chunks
½ tablespoon smoked paprika
2 garlic cloves, minced
4 ripe Roma tomatoes, diced
Juice of ½ lemon
Sea salt and pepper
Sandwich wraps, store-bought
1 medium head romaine lettuce, shredded
¼ cup fresh parsley, measured then roughly chopped

TO MAKE THE SPICY YOGURT:
In a small bowl, and using a rubber spatula, combine all ingredients until well incorporated. Allow to sit and marinate in refrigerator or at room temperature for at least 1 hour. Salt and pepper to taste.

TO MAKE THE WRAPS:
Preheat the oven to 350°F.

Place a large heavy sauté pan over medium-high heat and add the olive oil. Once the oil is hot, reduce the heat to medium, add the cumin and allow to become aromatic, about 1 minute.

Add the eggplant, smoked paprika, and garlic, stirring constantly, 7 to 8 minutes, until the eggplant is soft. Reduce the heat to low, add the diced tomatoes, and cover for 1 minute. Add the lemon juice and mash the eggplant with a fork. The eggplant should be a good mixture of chunky and smooth. Remove from the heat and season with salt and pepper to taste.

Lightly wet a tea towel (it should be wet but not dripping) and place the sandwich wraps in the middle of the towel and fold over to create a bundle. Place bundle on a baking sheet. Allow the wraps to warm in oven for 5 to 10 minutes, until soft and pliable.

To serve, place desired amount of spicy yogurt in a line across the middle of a wrap, place romaine lettuce on top of yogurt, and top with eggplant. Add another dollop of spicy yogurt across the eggplant, and sprinkle with fresh parsley. Roll by first folding the bottom of the wrap over the fillings, then folding the sides in, then rolling from the bottom up to create a tight wrap.

Did I Buy a Falafel From You Yesterday?

All of the Greene sisters seem to have their own thing with Ross. If the youngest, Jill, isn't trying to date him, Amy, the middle sister, is so self-absorbed that she can't seem to figure out where she's met him before. "Did I buy a falafel from you yesterday?" she asks, when she goes to babysit her niece Ella . . . um, *Emma*.

GARLIC CRÈME FRAÎCHE:
18 ounces crème fraîche
2 garlic cloves, minced
Zest and juice of 1 lemon
Salt and pepper

FALAFEL:
1½ cups dried chickpeas
¼ cup parsley, measured and
    chopped
2 garlic cloves, minced
2 tablespoons chickpea flour
2 tablespoons ground cumin
2 tablespoons ground coriander
1 medium onion, chopped
Salt and pepper
4 cups vegetable oil

PITA SANDWICH:
6 to 12 pita breads
One 16-ounce container hummus
Beefsteak tomatoes, sliced in rounds
2 pounds assorted salad mix
Pickled Red Onion (page 15)

TO MAKE THE GARLIC CRÈME FRAÎCHE:
Blend the crème fraîche, garlic, and lemon juice a blender until smooth, 2 to 3 minutes. Fold in the lemon zest. Season with salt and pepper to taste. Transfer to a bowl, cover, and refrigerate for at least 2 hours. The garlic crème fraîche can be stored in the refrigerator for up to a week.

TO MAKE THE FALAFEL:
Soak the dry chickpeas in a medium to large bowl of water overnight. The water should come 1 to 2 inches above chickpeas. Chickpeas will absorb the water and expand in size.

Combine all the soaked chickpeas, parsley, garlic, chickpea flour, cumin, coriander, and onion in a food processor and pulse until a chunky paste forms. Do not overblend or else you will make hummus. Season with salt and pepper to taste. The mixture should be crumbly, but wet and able to hold together. If the falafels are too wet, add a little more chickpea flour. If they are too crumbly and falling apart, add a little water.

In a large heavy sauté pan, heat the oil over medium high until it reaches 300°F. While waiting for the oil to heat, begin to shape slightly flattened balls of falafel about 2 to 3 inches in diameter. Place on a baking sheet lined with parchment paper.

Once the oil is hot, reduce the heat to medium. Working in batches, place 3 or 4 falafel balls into the oil at a time. Cook until golden on one side, about 2 to 3 minutes, then flip and cook on the second side, another 2 to 3 minutes or until golden.

Using a spider strainer or a slotted spoon, remove the falafel balls from the oil, and place on a platter lined with paper towels. Fry the remaining falafels.

TO MAKE THE PITA SANDWICH:
To serve your falafel, slice a pita open one-quarter of the way through to open the pocket. Smear hummus on one side, and place 2 or 3 rounds of tomato on the other side.

Stuff the bottom of the pita with mixed greens, then place falafel on top of the greens and top with 3 to 5 rings of Pickled Red Onions.

Chandler's Grilled Cheese

Chandler and Thanksgiving just can't seem to get along. It all started with his parents announcing their divorce, and escalated when he was rushed to the emergency room because Monica severed his toe. If I were him, I'd steer clear of the holiday too. Rather than eating the traditional turkey dinner, he celebrates by eating delicious grilled cheese sandwiches. You don't need to wait for traumatizing life events to happen on Thanksgiving to eat these! You're welcome to substitute the tomato jam in this recipe with a store-bought version, but making your own is easy, tasty, and is also delicious on other recipes such as Monica's Meatloaf Sandwich (page 64) and Jam-and-a-Spoon Scones (page 147).

TOMATO JAM:
2 tablespoons ground cumin
2 pounds cherry tomatoes
1 teaspoon grated fresh ginger
Zest and juice of 1 lemon
1 cup brown sugar
1 cup water
1 medium onion, sliced
1 tablespoon vegetable oil

GRILLED CHEESE:
1 tablespoon olive oil
2 yellow onions, sliced
Butter, softened
1 sourdough loaf, cut into
   12 slices
24 slices cheese of your choice

TO MAKE THE TOMATO JAM:

In a medium heavy pot, combine all the ingredients and heat on high. Allow the mixture to come to a boil, stirring occasionally with a rubber spatula or wooden spoon.

Reduce the heat to low, and allow to simmer until the jam thickens, about 1 hour.

Place the jam in a sanitized jar that has a tight-fitting lid (such as a mason jar). Offset the lid on the jar, so that warm air can escape, and allow to sit until it reaches room temperature, 2 to 4 hours.

Screw on lid tightly and refrigerate for at least 4 hours. The jam can be kept in the refrigerator for up to 2 weeks.

TO MAKE THE GRILLED CHEESE:

Heat a large sauté pan over medium-high. Once hot, reduce the heat to medium and add the oil. Once oil is hot, add the onions and allow to cook, stirring occasionally, around 10 minutes. If onions are starting to burn, turn heat down to medium. Once browned and slightly caramelized, remove from the pan and set aside.

Wipe the pan clean with a paper towel, and place over medium heat.

Butter one side of each slice of bread. Flip every slice over so they are all butter-side-down on the work surface.

Next, smear a generous layer of tomato jam on half of the bread slices, then top with 1 or 2 tablespoons of caramelized onions. On the other bread slices, place 1 to 2 slices of cheese.

Working in batches, place the bread slices with the cheese butter-side down in the pan. Allow to toast for 2 to 3 minutes, until cheese is soft and melted and bread has browned a little.

Using a spatula, scoop up the bread slices with cheese, and place on top of the untoasted bread slice with the caramelized onions. Using your hand to steady the sandwich, use the spatula to transfer the whole sandwich back to the pan so the untoasted side is down. Allow the bread to toast for 2 to 3 minutes, until brown.

Give the sandwich a firm pat with the spatula, to make sure the cheese is sticking to the onions, and remove from heat and repeat with remaining sandwiches. Cut the sandwiches into squares, diagonals, or whatever shape the pilgrims didn't use. Enjoy!

Pizza and Pastas

Pizza Dough

Joey's Marinara Sauce

The Joey Special: Two Pizzas

G. Stephanopoulos's Pizza

Definitely Not Vegetarian Lasagna

Buffay the Vampire Layer's Vegetable Lasagna

Righteous Mac and Cheese

Estelle's One-Pan Pasta

PhilloSophie's Cajun Catfish Alfredo

Pizza Essentials

Pizza plays an essential part of the *Friends* series. Joey is always eating it, Rachel and Ross officially broke up while eating it, and it's safe to say that some of the Friends' most significant bonding moments have been over pizza. These basic recipes will get you set to make everyone's favorite, like The Joey Special: Two Pizzas (page 80)!

This recipe will produce enough dough for four 13-inch pizzas—which is enough for a pizza party—or you can freeze the rest for later.

Pizza Dough

YIELD: Four 13-inch pizzas
PREP TIME: 30 minutes

2½ cups warm water
3 tablespoons active dry yeast
⅓ cup olive oil, plus more for bowl
1 teaspoon salt
1½ teaspoons sugar
7 cups 00 flour or all-purpose flour

In a medium bowl, mix together the warm water and yeast. Allow to form bubbles, 3 to 5 minutes. Grease a large bowl with olive oil and set aside.

While the yeast is activating, mix the salt and sugar into flour in a second large bowl and create a well in the center of the flour. Once the yeast is activated, slowly pour the water and yeast mixture into the center of the well. Start combining the flour and water with your hands or a wooden spoon until the flour has become a shaggy dough.

Turn out the dough on a well-floured nonporous work surface, and begin to knead until the surface of the dough is smooth and firm, 12 to 15 minutes.

Place the kneaded dough into the bowl prepared with olive oil and give it a toss so that the dough is lightly coated with olive oil all over. Cover with a plastic wrap or a tea towel, and allow the dough to rise for 5 hours.

Once dough has risen, turn the dough out onto a nonporous surface, and punch it down to press out air bubbles.

Divide the dough into 4 pieces, and allow to rest for about 10 minutes. If baking immediately, now would be a good time to preheat the oven to 450°F. Otherwise, you can wrap the dough in plastic and freeze for later use.

A NOTE FROM CHEF MONICA:
00 flour is an Italian flour often used for making pasta and pizza. It's available online and in some specialty stores. If you can't track it down, you can substitute with all-purpose flour.

78

Joey's Marinara Sauce

YIELD: 1 gallon
PREP AND COOK TIME: 2 hours

When a network casting lady comes on to Joey, he's confused as to whether he has to sleep with her to get the part on a popular soap opera. When his agent Estelle confirms he does, he gets so stressed out, he makes enough marinara sauce to feed Italy. Who knew it would take so much sauce to become Dr. Drake Ramoray?

This sauce is great for both pizzas and pastas and will make enough for multiple applications.

5 pounds Roma tomatoes or two 28-ounce cans crushed or stewed tomatoes
2 tablespoons olive oil
1 large white onion, diced
Salt and pepper
⅓ cup basil, torn
⅓ cup oregano, finely chopped
⅓ cup fresh parsley, chopped
⅓ cup thyme, chopped
3 to 4 garlic cloves, minced
1 cup water (optional)
2 tablespoons honey (optional)

If using canned tomatoes, skip ahead to start cooking the onion. If using fresh tomatoes, gently cut an X in the bottom of each tomato, just deep enough to pierce the skin. Bring a large pot filled with water to a boil.

While the water is heating, fill a large bowl with ice cubes and water.

Once the water is boiling, add the tomatoes, and allow to cook until the skin begins to peel away from the tomato, about 1 minute. Remove the tomatoes and plunge into ice bath.

Cut the tomatoes into fourths, peel the skin off, and remove the seeds. Discard the skin and seeds, then set aside the tomato flesh.

Heat a large heavy saucepan on medium. Once hot, add the olive oil. Allow to heat, about 1 minute, and then add the onions. Sauté the onions until translucent and aromatic, 3 to 4 minutes. Season with salt and pepper to taste.

Add the tomato, basil, oregano, parsley, thyme, and garlic, season again with salt and pepper, then stir. Allow ingredients to come to a rolling boil, about 2 to 5 minutes, then reduce the heat to low. Allow to simmer for about 1 hour.

If the sauce is too thick, add the optional water. If sauce needs to be a bit less acidic, add the optional honey.

The Joey Special: Two Pizzas

Season 4, Episode 23
"The One With Ross's Wedding, Part 1"

YIELD: 6 servings or serves 1 Joey Tribbiani
PREP AND COOK TIME: 40 minutes

Joey has his own signature pizza order—it's called "The Joey Special." While we don't know specifically what type of pizzas he orders, we know he orders two. While in London, Joey calls Phoebe, and when he hears that she's ordered The Joey Special he gets homesick.

GARLIC AND CLAM PIZZA:
Pizza Dough (page 78)
1½ cups frozen clam meat, thawed
3 garlic cloves, finely minced
¾ cup grated Pecorino Romano cheese
⅓ cup fresh oregano, chopped
Olive oil

HAM SPREAD, SAUSAGE, AND SALAMI PIZZA:
Pizza Dough (page 78)
3 tablespoons Ham Spread (page 10)
½ cup Joey's Marinara Sauce (page 79) or store-bought
1 cup shredded mozzarella cheese
10 to 13 slices salami
1 cup Italian sausage, cooked and crumbled

TO MAKE THE GARLIC AND CLAM PIZZA:
Preheat the oven to 450°F. If using a pizza stone, place it in the oven to get hot. Roll out the pizza dough into a 13-inch circle. If using a pizza stone, place the dough on a pizza peel or wooden cutting board, otherwise assemble the pizza on a baking sheet.

In a small bowl, pat the clams dry and mix with the garlic. Spread garlic and clam mixture out evenly over the dough.

Top the pizza with the Pecorino Romano and fresh oregano. Drizzle with olive oil and brush the crust with a bit of olive oil.

Using the pizza peel or wooden cutting board, slide the pizza onto the heated pizza stone, or place the baking sheet in the oven, and cook until the cheese is bubbly and the crust is golden, 15 to 20 minutes.

TO MAKE THE HAM SPREAD, SAUSAGE, AND SALAMI PIZZA:
Preheat the oven to 450°F. If using a pizza stone, place it in the oven to get hot. Roll out the pizza dough into a 13-inch circle.

Spread the ham spread and marinara sauce evenly over the dough. Top with the mozzarella cheese, salami, and crumbled sausage.

Place the pizza on a baking sheet or a pizza stone that has been heating in the oven, and cook until the cheese is bubbly and the crust is golden, 15 to 20 minutes.

G. Stephanopoulos's Pizza

Season 1, Episode 4
"The One With George Stephanopoulos"

YIELD: 4 servings
PREP AND COOK TIME: 30 minutes

The girls are having a bad night, when they're accidentally delivered a pizza meant for George Stephanopoulos and things turn around. Not only do they get a peek into President Clinton's sexy campaign guy's culinary preferences, they spy on him across the street long enough to sneak a glimpse of even more (and he's no ugly naked guy!). Seems like fair repayment for getting G. Stephanopoulos's mushroom, green pepper, and onion instead of their fat-free crust with extra cheese.

Pizza Dough (page 78)
1 cup Joey's Marinara Sauce (page 79) or store-bought
1 cup shredded mozzarella cheese
8 ounces porcini or portobello mushrooms, sliced
1 green bell pepper, thinly sliced
Cherry tomatoes, halved
1 yellow onion, thinly sliced
Aleppo chile flakes or crushed red pepper flakes
Salt and pepper

Preheat the oven to 450°F. If using a pizza stone, place it in the oven to get hot. Roll out the pizza dough into a 13-inch circle. If using a pizza stone, place the dough on a pizza peel or wooden cutting board, otherwise assemble the pizza on a baking sheet.

Spread the marinara sauce evenly over the dough.

Top with the mozzarella cheese, followed by the mushrooms, green bell pepper, cherry tomatoes, and yellow onion. Sprinkle with a large pinch of Aleppo chile flakes or crushed red pepper flakes, and season with salt and pepper to taste.

Using the pizza peel or wooden cutting board, slide the pizza onto the pizza stone, or place the baking sheet in the oven, and cook until the cheese is bubbly and the crust is golden, 15 to 20 minutes.

Definitely Not Vegetarian Lasagna

YIELD:
6 to 8 servings

PREP AND COOK TIME:
1½ hours

This lasagna made with tangy marinara, melted mozzarella, and spicy Italian sausage is perfect for a crowd—just as long as your Aunt Syl didn't actually want *vegetarian* lasagnas for her party, that is.

One 15-ounce container ricotta cheese
2 eggs
⅓ cup parsley, chopped
1½ pounds Italian sausage, cooked and crumbled
5 cups Joey's Marinara Sauce (page 79) or store-bought
12 to 14 lasagna sheets, cooked according to the package instructions
2 cups shredded mozzarella cheese
Salt and pepper

Preheat the oven to 400°F.

In a medium bowl, stir together the ricotta, eggs, and parsley. Season with salt and pepper to taste. Set aside.

In a second medium bowl, mix together the Italian sausage and marinara.

Spread a thin layer of marinara along the bottom of an 8-by-10-inch baking dish, then arrange a single layer of cooked lasagna sheets lengthwise in dish. Cover with thin layer of the ricotta mixture. Ladle marinara and Italian sausage over the ricotta, and sprinkle the shredded mozzarella over marinara in an even layer.

Repeat the layers until the dish is filled and the top layer is lasagna noodles. At this point, cover the lasagna with a thin layer of marinara sauce and top with mozzarella cheese.

Place the baking dish on the oven's center rack, and cook until the top layer of cheese is bubbly and brown, about 30 minutes.

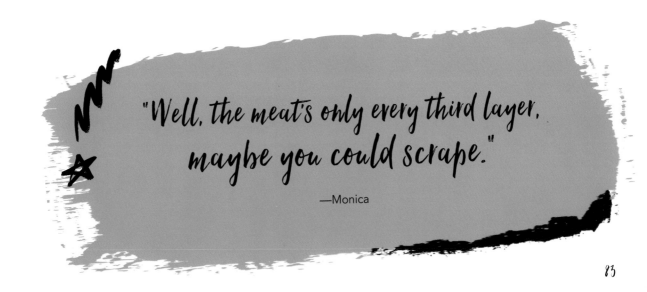

"Well, the meat's only every third layer, maybe you could scrape."

—Monica

Buffay the Vampire Layer's Vegetable Lasagna

YIELD: 6 to 8 servings
PREP AND COOK TIME: 1½ hours

Phoebe's identical twin, Ursula, isn't just walking around the city looking like Phoebe, she's also doing adult movies and garnering fans for both of them. Joey is hesitant to watch *Buffay the Vampire Layer* when he thinks it's Phoebe seducing "Nosfera-tool" on tape, but when an ankle tattoo IDs the actress as Ursula, he quickly changes his mind.

One 15-ounce container ricotta cheese

2 eggs

Zest and juice of ½ lemon

1½ tablespoons fresh thyme, measured and roughly chopped

Salt and pepper

3 tablespoons olive oil, divided

1 medium zucchini, diced small

4 cups spinach

1½ pounds cremini mushrooms, diced small

5 cups Joey's Marinara Sauce (page 79) or store-bought

12 to 14 lasagna noodles, cooked according to the package instructions

Shredded mozzarella cheese

In a medium bowl, stir together the ricotta, eggs, lemon zest, and thyme. Season with salt and pepper to taste. Set aside.

Heat a large pan on high. Once hot, reduce the heat to medium and add two tablespoons of the olive oil. Once the oil is shimmery, add the zucchini and spinach to the pan, give it one or two tosses, and cook until the moisture releases from the vegetables, about 3 minutes. Season with salt and pepper to taste. Remove the vegetables from the pan and set aside. Discard the vegetable liquid and reheat the pan.

Add the spinach and zucchini to ricotta mixture. Mix well, so that vegetables are incorporated and covered in ricotta.

Once the pan is hot again, add another tablespoon of olive oil to the pan, then add the cremini mushrooms and stir. Add in a squeeze of lemon juice, and season with salt and pepper to taste. Cook until the mushrooms are tender, about 3 minutes.

In a medium bowl, combine the mushrooms and the marinara sauce.

Preheat the oven to 400°F.

Spread a thin layer of marinara along the bottom of an 8-by-10-inch baking dish, then arrange a single layer of cooked lasagna sheets lengthwise in dish. Cover with a thin layer of ricotta mixture. Ladle the marinara and mushroom over the ricotta, and cover the marinara with some of the shredded mozzarella.

Repeat the layers until the top layer is lasagna noodles. At this point, cover the lasagna with a thin layer of marinara sauce and top with mozzarella cheese.

Place the baking dish on the oven's center rack, and cook until the top layer of cheese is bubbly and brown, about 30 minutes.

Righteous Mac and Cheese

Season 5, Episode 8
"The One With All the Thanksgivings"

YIELD: 6 servings
PREP AND COOK TIME: 40 minutes

It's Thanksgiving 1987, and Monica is eagerly trying to get the attention of Ross's friend Chandler. Chandler hates Thanksgiving and refuses to eat anything that the pilgrims may have eaten, so Monica offers to make him mac and cheese. Indifferent to Monica's advances, he agrees. When Monica sits next to him on the couch and asks how he likes the mac and cheese, he quips, "Yeah, it's great. You should become a chef." Of course, he doesn't mean it, but in desperation, Monica takes his advice and the rest is *Friends* history.

12 ounces dried elbow macaroni pasta
¼ cup (½ stick) butter, plus more for pasta water
1 tablespoon mustard powder
½ tablespoon garlic powder
1 tablespoon Creole seasoning or dry barbecue rub seasoning
¼ cup all-purpose flour
One 12-ounce can evaporated milk
2 cups half-and-half or 1 cup heavy whipping cream and 1 cup whole milk
2 cups shredded sharp cheddar cheese (reserve ¼ cup)
1 cup shredded Gruyère cheese (reserve ¼ cup)
Salt and pepper

Bring a large pot of water to a boil. Add the elbow macaroni and a small pat of butter, and cook until al dente, about 10 minutes. Drain in a colander and place back into the pot off heat without rinsing.

In a large pan on medium heat, melt the ¼ cup butter. Once melted, stir in the mustard powder, garlic powder, Creole or barbecue seasoning, and flour to create a roux. Once the roux reaches a blond, almost brown color, 3 to 5 minutes, remove from the heat. Slowly whisk in the evaporated milk. Try not to create any lumps.

Place pan back on the heat, and reduce the heat to medium-low. Pour in the half-and-half, or heavy whipping cream and milk, and continue to whisk, making sure to whisk the bottom of the pan, until a béchamel forms, 3 to 5 minutes. The béchamel should begin to become thick like a potato soup in consistency, but not as thick as a milkshake. If too thick, remove from the heat and stir in more half-and-half.

Add the cheddar and Gruyère cheese, and stir until incorporated and the sauce is cheesy, about 2 minutes. Season with salt and pepper to taste.

Preheat the oven to 375°F.

Pour béchamel sauce over the cooked pasta. Using a figure eight motion, turn the pasta into the béchamel until evenly coated. Season with salt and pepper to taste.

Transfer the pasta mixture into a large ceramic or glass baking dish, top with the remaining cheese, and bake until the cheese becomes bubbly, and the cheese in the corners of the dish forms a crust, 10 to 15 minutes.

Estelle's One-Pan Pasta

YIELD:
2 to 4 servings

PREP AND COOK TIME:
20 minutes

Joey's agent Estelle may not be able to land him anything more than two-line roles as a taxi driver, or as Al Pacino's butt double, but her heart is in the right place—even if lipstick is constantly on her teeth. But she eventually gets Joey the role as Dr. Ramoray on a popular soap opera, and she does know a thing or two about eating on a budget. God rest her soul! If you're strapped for cash while you look for your next gig, try this budget-friendly one-pan pasta.

12 ounces dry bucatini or spaghetti
12 ounces cherry tomatoes, halved
3 garlic cloves, thinly sliced
1½ tablespoons Calabrian chile paste or crushed red pepper flakes
3 to 4 sprigs basil, torn, plus more for serving
3 tablespoons olive oil
4½ cups water
Salt and pepper
16 pieces 16/20 shrimp, cleaned (optional)
Juice of ½ lemon (optional)
¼ cup grated Parmesan cheese

In a large heavy pan with high sides (such as a sauté pan), lay the dry pasta flat. Add the tomatoes, garlic, Calabrian chile paste or crushed red pepper flakes, and torn basil. Drizzle the ingredients with the olive oil, then add the water and a generous pinch of salt.

Turn the heat on medium-high, and allow water to come to a boil, stirring constantly with tongs, for 10 to 12 minutes. The sauce should begin to thicken as the tomatoes break down, and the pasta should become al dente.

If you've landed an acting gig, and can afford to splurge, add the shrimp directly into the liquid 3 to 5 minutes before pasta is done. The shrimp is done when it is light pink on both sides, and without any traces of being translucent or gray. Take the pan off the heat, squeeze in the lemon juice, and gently toss to incorporate. If you're still struggling for your big break, just omit the shrimp.

Plate your pasta and finish with a generous amount of Parmesan, freshly ground black pepper, and fresh basil.

"After all your years of struggling, you're finally been able to crack your way into show business."

—Chandler

PhilloSophie's Cajun Catfish Alfredo

Season 2, Episode 5
"The One With Five Steaks and an Eggplant"

YIELD: 6 servings
PREP AND COOK TIME: 2½ hours

When Monica is promoted, the Friends go out for a celebratory meal at the fancy restaurant PhilloSophie—but Joey, Rachel, and Phoebe can't afford full entrées like Chandler's cajun catfish or Monica and Ross's carpaccio and grilled prawns. Instead of going out for a meal that might break the bank, treat your friends to a delicious home-cooked meal that would fit right in on the menu at that upscale restaurant.

CAJUN CATFISH:
1 teaspoon black pepper
1½ teaspoons paprika
1 tablespoon onion powder
1 teaspoon garlic powder
1 tablespoon dried oregano
1 tablespoon dried thyme
1 teaspoon cayenne pepper
Six 4-ounce catfish fillets
⅓ cup buttermilk
Salt
2 tablespoons sunflower oil

ALFREDO SAUCE:
⅓ cup unsalted butter
1½ cups heavy cream
2 garlic cloves, finely minced
1 cup grated Romano cheese
Freshly ground black pepper

PASTA:
1½ pounds dry fettuccini pasta
1 tablespoon olive oil
1 to 2 large heads broccoli, cut into florets
Fresh parsley, roughly chopped

TO MAKE THE CAJUN CATFISH:
In a small bowl, mix together the black pepper, paprika, onion powder, garlic powder, oregano, thyme, and cayenne pepper. Set aside.

Place the catfish in a medium bowl. Drizzle buttermilk over the fish and toss until well coated. Cover both sides in the seasoning mixture. Allow to marinate in refrigerator for 1 to 2 hours. In the meantime, prepare the alfredo sauce.

Once marinated and after making the alfredo sauce and cooking the pasta (see below), heat a large nonstick pan on medium. Once hot, working in batches, add the sunflower oil and place the fish skin-side up in the pan. Allow to blacken, 2 to 3 minutes, and flip to cook on the skin side, 3 minutes longer.

TO MAKE THE ALFREDO SAUCE:
Thirty minutes before cooking the catfish, combine all the alfredo sauce ingredients in a large pot. Heat on medium-high. Stir until the ingredients are incorporated and alfredo sauce begins to thicken, 10 to 15 minutes. Keep the heat on low and stir occasionally as you prepare the other components.

TO MAKE THE PASTA:
While sauce is thickening, heat a large pot of water on high and cook the fettuccine according to package's instructions. Once al dente, remove the pasta from the liquid but do not turn off the heat. Toss the pasta in the olive oil.

A NOTE FROM CHEF MONICA:
Al dente means "to the tooth," and refers to cooking the pasta until it's nearly done but still has a slight firmness when you bite into it.

Return the pasta water to a rolling boil then place broccoli florets into water and allow to blanch, about 3 minutes or until florets turn a vibrant green. Fill a large bowl with water and ice, then drain the broccoli and plunge into the ice-cold water.

TO ASSEMBLE:
Toss the fettucine in the alfredo sauce until the pasta is well coated. Drain the broccoli and gently fold half of the florets into the sauce and pasta. Generously plate the pasta, stacking the pasta high. Stagger 3 to 4 freshly blanched broccoli florets on each pasta mound. Generously season with freshly ground black pepper, and top each mound with 1 piece of blackened catfish. Sprinkle with fresh parsley.

Main Dishes

Rachel's Famous Baked Potato and Diet Cola

Half a Shepherd's Pie

Monica's Onion Galette

Blue Fingernail in the Quiche

Ugly Naked Guy's Sausage Party

God Bless the Chickpea Shakshuka

The Importance of Unagi:
Crispy Salmon Skin Poke Bowls

Carol and Susan's Bricked Chicken
Breasts With Creamy Polenta

Bathtub Fried Chicken

Ross's Hand-Scalding Fajitas

The One With the Picnic Basket (Duck Rillettes)

Phoebe's Pregnancy Steak

Allesandro's Bouillabaisse

Rachel's Famous Baked Potato and Diet Cola

YIELD:
2 servings

PREP AND COOK TIME:
1½ hours

If you're anything like Rachel, the finer things in life don't have to be complicated—well, unless it comes to your love life, then that's always complicated. If you don't have a chef friend who can cook you a meal to impress a crush, try these simple and yet wonderfully dressed baked potatoes. I don't recommend pairing them with a diet cola, but Rachel sure does!

The caviar makes this recipe a luxe presentation, but can easily be omitted. Serve with Rachel's Side Salad (page 53) for a complete meal, and add some Brown Bird Holiday Macarons (page 144) for dessert.

2 russet potatoes, washed and scrubbed
2 tablespoons olive oil
¼ cup flaky sea salt
8 ounces crème fraîche
¼ cup fresh dill, stemmed, measured, and roughly chopped, plus 2 sprigs for garnishing
Freshly ground black pepper
¼ cup caviar or fish roe
½ small lemon, cut into wedges

Preheat the oven to 350°F.

Using a fork, prick the potatoes all over.

Place the potatoes in a medium bowl and coat with olive oil. Make sure they are well coated. Season the skin generously with flaky sea salt.

Place the potatoes directly on the oven rack and bake for 60 to 75 minutes, until the skin is crisp and a fork can easily be inserted all the way through the potatoes.

While the potatoes are baking, mix together the crème fraîche and dill in a small bowl, and season with salt and pepper to taste. Stir until well incorporated. Place in refrigerator.

Once potatoes are done, slice horizontally and fill with the crème fraîche and dill mixture. Top each potato with caviar, and add a fresh sprig of dill on top for garnish. Serve with freshly ground black pepper and a lemon wedge. Enjoy, Honey!

Half a Shepherd's Pie

Season 6, Episode 9
"The One Where Ross Got High"

YIELD: 6 servings
PREP AND COOK TIME: 1½ hours

The good thing about this recipe is that it doesn't include a recipe for half a traditional English trifle, which is a layered dessert. When Rachel botches her attempt at a Thanksgiving dessert, she serves half a trifle and half a shepherd's pie to create a dish that only Joey has a taste for. Instead, we recommend you serve these individual pies as a wonderful entrée. Don't confuse this with Rachel's Meat Trifle (page 163) and combine the two—-otherwise, it will most assuredly taste like feet.

This recipe is meant to be served in individual 6-inch pie dishes or ramekins, but it can easily fill a larger baking dish.

1 tablespoon sunflower oil
1 large yellow onion, chopped
Salt and pepper
2 large carrots, peeled and chopped
1½ pounds lean ground beef
1½ cups frozen peas
1 tablespoon Worcestershire sauce
2 tablespoons fresh rosemary,
   measured then finely chopped
1 cup beef stock
4 ounces tomato paste
3 to 4 cups Mashed Potatoes
   (page 130)

Heat a large heavy pan or skillet on high. Once hot, add the oil. Once oil is shimmery, add the onions and sauté until they start to become translucent, 2 to 3 minutes. Season with salt and pepper to taste.

Add in the carrots and allow to caramelize, 2 to 3 minutes.

Push onions and carrots off to one side of the pan, add the ground beef, and cook until brown, 3 to 5 minutes. Season with salt and pepper to taste.

Once the meat is browned, add the peas, Worcestershire sauce, rosemary, beef stock, and tomato paste. Stir and reduce the heat to medium-low. Allow to simmer until the stock reduces by half, about 15 minutes. Season again with salt and pepper to taste.

Preheat the oven to 375°F.

Divide the meat mixture between six 6-inch individual serving pie tins. Top with a generous portion of mashed potatoes and spread the mashed potatoes to cover the meat. Place on a baking tray.

Bake until the mashed potatoes are golden brown, 10 to 15 minutes.

Monica's Onion Galette

When Monica is interviewing for a chef job at a restaurant owned by one of Phoebe's massage clients, Phoebe brings him over for dinner as an interview. The problem? He's been smoking doobies all the way there in the cab. This onion galette is more satiating than the small bite-sized tartlets Monica offers her potential boss. Though "galette" is not quite as fun to say as "tartlets," this galette is sure to impress anyone, even if they're baked.

1 recipe Pie Crust dough (page 12), refrigerated
3 tablespoons canola oil
6 to 8 medium yellow onions, cut into ½-inch slices
2 tablespoons fresh oregano, measured and roughly chopped
Salt and pepper
½ tablespoon sherry vinegar
¾ cup shredded Gruyère cheese
1 egg

Preheat the oven to 425°F and line 2 or 3 baking sheets with parchment paper.

Remove dough from the refrigerator, and roll into two 13-inch rounds. Place the rounds on the prepared baking sheets, and place back in the fridge.

Heat a large heavy pot or cast-iron pan on high. Once hot, reduce the heat to medium and add the oil. Once oil is glistening, add in the onions, oregano, and salt and pepper to taste. Allow the onions to caramelize, stirring occasionally, 10 to 12 minutes. Add the sherry vinegar.

Once onions are done, pull out the pie dough, and working from the center of each round outward, sprinkle the onions over the dough, being sure to leave about 2 inches around the edge clean to fold in for a crust.

Sprinkle the Gruyère over the onion, then create the crust by folding the 2-inch uncovered edge up over the filling. Continue folding the crust around the galette, overlapping the dough edges as you work.

Lightly beat 1 egg in a small bowl, and wash the crust in egg using a pastry brush.

Bake for about 20 minutes until the crust is crisp and the cheese is melted and slightly bubbly. Try not to be impatient and eat taco shells while you wait!

"Tartlets! Tartlets! Tartlets!
The word has lost all meaning."

—Steve

Blue Fingernail in the Quiche

YIELD:
6 servings

PREP AND COOK TIME:
1 hour

Monica caters a lunch for her mom and some of her friends. But while preparing the meal, she accidentally loses a fake blue fingernail in the quiche. Always expecting to be disappointed by Monica, Mrs. Geller has backup lasagna ready in the freezer as a plan B. Don't worry—the blue potatoes in this quiche are completely safe and delicious to eat!

1 cup purple potatoes, diced in 1-inch pieces
1 recipe Pie Crust dough (page 12)
2 cups dried beans (for blind-baking)
6 eggs
½ cup whole milk
½ cup cream
Salt and pepper
½ medium leek, sliced
1 cup shredded Gruyère cheese, divided

Preheat the oven to 375°F.

In a large pot, add potatoes and water and heat on high until they begin to boil. Allow to partially boil, until potatoes are softer, but not fully cooked, about 10 minutes. Once par-boiled, drain and set aside.

Roll out the pie dough large enough to fit a 10-inch pie dish. Place the dough in the pie dish, and layer with a large sheet of parchment paper. Pour the dried beans over the parchment paper, and blind-bake until crust is partially cooked, 10 to 12 minutes. Set aside.

While the crust is blind-baking, in a medium bowl, beat together the eggs, milk, and cream. Season with salt and pepper. Add the potatoes, leeks, and ¾ cup of the Gruyère into the egg and cream mixture.

When pie crust is done blind baking, grab all four corners of the parchment paper and remove the beans and save for reuse. Pour the egg and potato mixture directly into the crust. Top with the last ¼ cup of Gruyère and bake until the crust and egg mixture are golden brown, about 40 to 45 minutes.

A NOTE FROM CHEF MONICA:
Blind-baking means baking a crust without filling first, usually with pie weights or dry, uncooked beans to keep it from rising. The beans can be reused to blind-bake another pie crust, but should not be cooked and eaten.

Ugly Naked Guy's Sausage Party

The gang was obsessed with spying on their neighbor, Ugly Naked Guy. When Joey notices that Ugly Naked Guy is unusually still, they worry that he has died and fashion a giant poking device out of chopsticks to try and poke him for signs of life. He is alive, but less than thrilled with their antics. To celebrate Ugly Naked Guy's ongoing vitality, this sausage party has something for everyone. Cook enough sausages for a crowd, then offer three different kinds of toppings for a feast. If you have friends who don't eat anything with a face, be sure to include some vegetarian sausages.

18 sausages of choice
18 hot dog buns

ELOTE DOGS:
2 tablespoons milk
1 tablespoon salt
2 ears corn
2 lime wedges
1 cup cilantro, divided
5 ounces Tajín seasoning
One 6-ounce jar mayonnaise
½ cup Pickled Red Onion (page 15)
10 ounces cotija or feta cheese

KIMCHI DOGS:
2 garlic cloves
½ cup mayonnaise
Salt and pepper
One 16-ounce jar kimchi
½ cup Crispy Shallots (page 15) or
    store-bought crunchy onions

SOUTHERN DOGS:
4 ounces Dijon mustard
3 cups Righteous Mac and Cheese
    (page 85)
One 16-ounce jar dill pickle spears
Prepared barbecue sauce

On a hot grill, cook the pork or beef sausages until they reach an internal temperature of 145°F. If they are poultry sausages, cook until they reach an internal temperature of 165°F. If a grill is unavailable, boil the sausages until they are cooked through, 7 to 10 minutes. Drain and then brown on each side in a large hot skillet on medium heat to add color. Place on a large platter. If using vegetarian sausage in conjunction with meat sausages, be sure to cook and plate them separately.

Preheat the oven to 200°F. Five minutes before serving, warm the hot dog buns in the oven for about 5 minutes.

TO MAKE ELOTE DOGS:
Bring a large pot of water to a boil. Once the water is boiling, add the milk, salt, and corn. Allow the corn to cook until it turns bright yellow, 4 to 5 minutes. Drain and set aside.

Set a grill or griddle on high. Once hot, place the corn on the griddle or grill. Grill on each side about 2 minutes, allowing grill marks to form.

Using a sharp knife, cut the corn off the cob. Mix the kernels with lime juice, ½ cup cilantro, and Tajín, and place in a serving bowl.

Into individual small bowls, add remaining sausage toppings: mayonnaise, pickled red onions, and remaining ½ cup cilantro.

To assemble, place mayonnaise on one or both sides of the hot dog bun. Place a sausage in the bun. Top with elote corn and a sprinkle of cotija or feta cheese.

TO MAKE KIMCHI DOGS:
In a food processor, combine the garlic and mayonnaise until well incorporated, about 2 minutes. Add salt and pepper to taste.

Place the kimchi and crispy shallots toppings in serving bowls.

> *"We're fashioning a very long poking device."*
>
> —Joey

To assemble, spread a desired amount of garlic mayonnaise on both sides of a hot dog bun. Place a sausage in the bun. Top with a generous amount of kimchi and crispy shallots.

TO MAKE SOUTHERN DOGS:
Place all the toppings in serving bowls.

To assemble, spread a thin layer of mustard on the inside of a hot dog bun. Place a sausage inside the bun. Wedge a pickle on one or both sides of the sausage. Top with a spoonful of mac and cheese, and drizzle with barbecue sauce.

God Bless the Chickpea Shakshuka

YIELD:
6 servings

PREP AND COOK TIME:
45 minutes

God bless the chickpea! Chickpeas can do a lot of things: They can become a creamy, garlicky hummus, and with a little elbow grease, they can even become a delicious breakfast dish that both your vegetarian and non-vegetarian friends will love. Sadly, they probably won't be able to save a date with a couple of cute doctors that's going poorly because you and your friend lied about your identity so your friend could use your insurance. Serve with warm flatbreads and dollops of labneh (thick Middle Eastern yogurt) or crumbled feta cheese.

¼ cup avocado oil
1 medium yellow onion, diced
1 teaspoon sweet paprika
1½ tablespoons ground cumin
3 tablespoons harissa
3 tablespoons tomato paste
4 garlic cloves, minced
One 24-ounce can plain (no basil)
   San Marzano tomatoes, crushed
One 16-ounce can chickpeas
Salt and pepper
6 eggs (optional)
¼ cup parsley, chopped

Heat a large heavy skillet on medium-high. Once hot, reduce heat to medium and add avocado oil and diced onions. Stir and allow onions to sauté until translucent, about 5 minutes.

Add the paprika and cumin and allow the spices to become aromatic, 2 to 3 minutes, stirring occasionally.

Stir in the harissa and tomato paste so that the onion and spices begin to form a paste.

Place the minced garlic directly on top of onion paste and gently stir into the mixture. Avoid direct heat with the garlic, as you don't want it to burn.

Add the crushed tomatoes and chickpeas, and reduce the heat to medium-low. Allow to simmer for about 10 minutes, until the shakshuka has thickened some. Add salt and pepper to taste.

If using eggs, crack them whole into evenly spaced divots in the shakshuka 3 minutes into simmering. Do not stir; allow them to cook in the tomato juice.

Before serving, garnish with freshly chopped parsley. Allow friends to serve themselves directly from the pan.

The Importance of Unagi: Crispy Salmon Skin Poke Bowls

According to Ross, the importance of unagi is "total awareness." Ross tries to teach Rachel and Phoebe, who are taking self-defense classes, the importance of unagi by hiding and trying to scare them in an attempt to catch them unaware and off guard. "Only by achieving true unagi can one be prepared for any danger that may befall you," he tells them. Meanwhile, the girls relentlessly try to tell him that *unagi* is the Japanese word for freshwater eel. We'll leave eel to the sushi pros, but that doesn't excuse you from preparing yourself for the complete awesomeness of these crispy salmon skin poke bowls.

2 cups sushi rice, rinsed

3 cups water

½ cup rice wine vinegar, divided

3 tablespoons sugar

½ cup cornstarch

Salt and pepper

2 pounds skin-on sushi-grade salmon fillet

¼ cup soy sauce or tamari

2 tablespoons chile paste

2 tablespoons brown sugar

2 cups vegetable oil

3 avocados, pitted and sliced

1 large cucumber, horizontally halved and sliced

1 cup edamame, shelled

1 cup seaweed salad, store-bought (optional)

¼ cup pickled ginger

2 stalks green onions, thinly sliced

¼ cup black sesame seeds, toasted

1 bottle prepared sriracha mayonnaise (optional)

Combine 2 cups sushi rice with 3 cups water in a medium saucepan and bring to a boil over high heat. Once boiling, reduce heat to low, cover, and let cook for 20 minutes. Rice should be tender by now. If it is not, add a tablespoon of hot water and allow to steam a few minutes more. Remove from heat and let cool.

In a medium bowl, mix ¼ cup of the rice vinegar and the sugar. Stir until the sugar dissolves. Set aside.

Place cornstarch in a small bowl and season with salt and pepper to taste. Set aside.

Next, dampen a tea towel, and place it underneath a cutting board; this will help hold the board in place. Place the salmon on the board. Using a sharp fish knife, grab fish by the tail end and make a small angled cut through the flesh. Slide the knife along the skin, as you hold the end firmly. The knife should slide down the skin, and remove it from the flesh. It's okay if a bit of meat is still on the skin. Set the flesh aside.

In a medium bowl, place the soy sauce or tamari, remaining ¼ cup rice vinegar, chile paste, and brown sugar. Gently stir until the sugar is dissolved.

Medium dice the salmon flesh and place in a bowl with soy sauce mixture. Toss evenly and allow to marinate, 5 to 7 minutes.

Heat the oil in a medium-sized deep frying pan on medium-high to 300°F. Then reduce the heat to medium.

Once oil is hot, begin to generously coat salmon skin on both sides in cornstarch. Drop the skin in the oil, and flip after 2 to 3 minutes. Test the skin for crispiness by rubbing a chopstick along the skin. If the skin sounds

"Ah, salmon skin roll."

—Rachel

scratchy and is firm, it is done. Remove from heat and set on a plate lined with paper towels. Slice the skin into ¼-inch-thick matchsticks.

In a large bowl, place the cooked and cooled rice. Pour the vinegar and sugar mixture over the rice, and gently toss. Try not to mash the rice.

To assemble, divide the rice among six bowls or plates. Add salmon on one side of the bowl, and avocado slices on the other. Fill empty spaces with cucumber, edamame, seaweed salad, and pickled ginger. Stick a few pieces of crispy salmon skin upright in the rice next to the salmon. Garnish with black sesame seeds and green onion. Drizzle with sriracha mayo, if using, and yell, "UNAGI!"

Carol and Susan's Bricked Chicken Breasts With Creamy Polenta

Season 2, Episode 11
"The One With the Lesbian Wedding"

YIELD: 2 servings
PREP AND COOK TIME: 1½ hours
INACTIVE TIME: 4 hours

When Carol and Susan's caterer has a mountain bike accident and ends up in a full-body cast, they ask Monica to cater their wedding reception. When trying to plan the menu, she can't decide between lamb or duck but in an attempt to be cute suggests chicken breasts instead.

You can always serve this dish with Wedding Pigs in a Blanket (page 37)—after all, Joey wrapped them himself. "Bricked" chicken involves cooking the chicken under a foil-wrapped brick. You can just as easily use a heavy skillet instead.

2 boneless chicken breasts

2 tablespoons sunflower oil, divided

1 tablespoon garlic powder

¼ teaspoon ground cardamom

½ teaspoon smoked paprika

2 cups chicken stock, divided

1 cup water

1 cup polenta

Salt and pepper

½ cup white wine

⅓ cup heavy cream

½ cup grated Parmesan cheese

Zest and juice of 1 orange

3 saffron threads (optional)

⅓ cup unsalted butter, cut into small pats

⅓ cup pitted green olives

2 tablespoons roughly chopped fresh parsley

In a container with a fitted lid, add the chicken breasts and 1 tablespoon of the sunflower oil. Make sure that chicken is well coated. Sprinkle garlic powder, cardamom, and smoked paprika over chicken breasts and toss until they are evenly covered in spices. Allow to marinate in the refrigerator for 4 hours.

In a medium pot, bring 1½ cups of the chicken stock and the water to a boil. Add the polenta while vigorously stirring with a whisk so that it doesn't clump. Reduce the heat to low and cook, uncovered, stirring occasionally, until the polenta is no longer coarse, 5 to 7 minutes. Cover and let stand off heat while you make the rest of the meal.

Heat a large heavy skillet on high. Once hot, add the remaining 1 tablespoon sunflower oil and heat until shimmery, about 1 minute. Reduce the heat to medium. Place the chicken skin-side down on the skillet and place a large foil-wrapped brick over the chicken breasts. Alternately, you can also add a layer of foil over the chicken and place a second heavy skillet on top. Be sure to turn an overhead fan on or open the windows, as the paprika will cause the air to get a little smoky. Once the skin is golden and crisp, about 5 minutes, flip and cook on the other side until the chicken reaches an internal temperature of 165°F in the thickest part of the meat, about 3 to 5 minutes longer.

Transfer the chicken to a cutting board, add salt and pepper to taste, then set chicken aside to rest. Reduce the heat under the pan to medium. Add the white wine to deglaze the pan, stirring to bring up the brown bits on the bottom of the pan. Then stir in heavy cream and Parmesan cheese.

Next, add the remaining ½ cup chicken stock, orange zest and juice, and saffron, and allow to simmer and reduce by half, 5 to 7 minutes. After the sauce has reduced, while stirring constantly, begin to add small pats of butter, until the sauce thickens, about 5 minutes. Once the sauce is thick, add the green olives with a bit of the juice from the jar, and season with salt and pepper to taste.

To serve, place a scoop of polenta on the bottom of the plate. Top with chicken breast and generously spoon sauce over the chicken, being sure to include some green olives. Garnish with freshly chopped parsley.

Bathtub Fried Chicken

Season 5, Episode 1
"The One With All the Kissing"

YIELD: 2 servings
PREP AND COOK TIME: 3 hours
INACTIVE TIME: 6 to 12 hours

Romantic candlelit dinners are a thing of the past! If you really like your sweetie, try a romantic candlelit bath, and pair it with fried chicken. Greasy fingers won't be an issue and your "friend that you care a lot about and want to spend more time with" will look so cute in bubbles! Serve with Magic Beans (page 55) and Kale Slaw (page 57) for a complete bathtub feast.

4 cups buttermilk
4 tablespoons garlic powder, divided
4 tablespoons mustard powder, divided
½ cup Old Bay Seasoning or dry rub barbecue seasoning, divided
Hot sauce, to taste, plus more for serving
One 3- to 4-pound whole chicken, cut into 6 pieces
4 cups canola oil
2 cups all-purpose flour
1 cup cornstarch
Salt and pepper
Honey for serving

A NOTE FROM CHEF MONICA:

If you are pairing this with the kale slaw, you can prepare the salad a day ahead, as well as while the chicken is marinating.

In a large bowl, combine the buttermilk, 2 tablespoons of the garlic powder, 2 tablespoons of the mustard powder, ¼ cup of the Old Bay or barbecue seasoning, and hot sauce. Mix well, then add the chicken pieces. Be sure the chicken is completely submerged in buttermilk mixture. Cover with a lid and allow to marinate in the refrigerator 6 to 12 hours or overnight.

One hour before serving, take the chicken out of the refrigerator and allow to rest at room temperature.

In a large cast-iron skillet or a medium heavy pot, heat the oil on medium high until it reaches 375°F. Preheat the oven to 400°F.

In a second large bowl, mix together the flour, cornstarch, and the remaining 2 tablespoons garlic powder, 2 tablespoons mustard powder, and the ¼ cup of Old Bay or barbecue seasoning. Add a generous amount of salt and pepper to taste. Taste a small amount of the flour mixture to make sure that it is seasoned well. It's okay if it's a little too seasoned, as frying the chicken will make it lose a bit of its saltiness.

Working with 2 pieces of chicken at a time, place the marinated chicken in the dry flour mixture. Make sure that the chicken is coated in every nook and cranny, and then immerse the chicken in hot oil. Fry 3 to 4 minutes on each side, for a total of 6 to 8 minutes, until the skin is golden brown.

The chicken should be golden brown on the outside and 165°F when a meat thermometer is inserted in the thickest part of the meat. If the chicken is still not up to temperature on the inside, place it on a wire baking rack over a baking sheet, and put it in the preheated oven. Allow the chicken to finish cooking while you fry the rest of the chicken pieces.

When ready to serve, line a serving tray or shallow dish with a tea towel, and pile high. Eat with your favorite hot sauce or a drizzle of honey!

Ross's Hand-Scalding Fajitas

YIELD:
6 servings

PREP AND COOK TIME:
30 minutes

What's more uncomfortable than an evening with your girlfriend, your ex-girlfriend (who's also the mother of your child) who's now dating your best friend, and said best friend? Drinking so many margaritas you pick up the hot dish of fajitas without oven mitts! Ross, it turns out, is not fine. Use of oven mitts when making these shrimp fajitas is highly recommended. Serve with The Ross-a-Tron (page 173) and Chick and the Duck Fat Black Beans (page 56).

1 tablespoon extra-virgin olive oil
12 ounces flank steak, thinly sliced
1 large red bell pepper, cut into
 ½-inch strips
1 large green bell pepper, cut into
 ½-inch strips
1 large red onion, sliced
¼ teaspoon ground cumin
¼ teaspoon chili powder
Salt and pepper
Juice of 1 lime
12 flour or corn tortillas
Cilantro, roughly chopped
Cotija cheese, crumbled
1 medium radish, thinly sliced and
 held in cold water
2 limes, cut into wedges
8 ounces Salsa Verde (page 29) or
 store-bought (optional)

Preheat the oven to 450°F.

In a large bowl, add the oil, steak, red bell pepper, green bell pepper, onion, cumin, chili powder, ½ teaspoon salt, ½ teaspoon pepper, and lime juice, and gently toss until everything is well coated in oil and spices. Set aside.

Wrap tortillas tightly in foil and place on the upper corner of half of a baking sheet.

On the other half of the baking sheet, spread the meat and vegetables.

Place the baking tray on the oven's middle rack and bake 12 minutes, or until the veggies are soft and the steak has browned on the outside.

To assemble, place meat and vegetables inside the tortillas. Top with a sprinkle of cilantro, cotija cheese, radish slices, a squeeze of lime juice and salsa verde if using.

"Fajitas! Be Careful! Very hot plate! Very hot!"

—Ross

The One With the Picnic Basket (Duck Rillettes)

If you're in love with love like Ross, and you want to convey deep feelings for a special Valentine or celebrate a monumental occasion like your one-year anniversary, pack a picnic basket that does it all. This duck rillette (a cold spread served like pâté), Cherry Couscous With Brown Butter (page 59), Pickled Greene Tomatoes (page 58), and Melanie's Fruit Salad (page 54) are a rich labor of love that's worth every bite. But maybe you shouldn't show up to your girlfriend's place of work with it when she's in the middle of a crucial deadline. Also it's probably not a good idea to sleep with Chloe from the Xerox place because you think you're on a break.

To make the rillettes, you'll need two sanitized glass jars with lids.

¼ cup coarse sea salt

2 tablespoons dried thyme

3 bay leaves

3 pounds duck legs, patted dry

4 cups duck or chicken stock

4 whole garlic cloves, peeled

1 bunch fresh thyme, divided, half destemmed

½ inch fresh ginger, sliced

2 tablespoons whole black peppercorns, plus freshly ground black pepper

3 tablespoons brandy

1 tablespoon Dijon mustard

Zest of 1 medium orange, plus more for garnishing

½ cup parsley, chopped

Crackers or baguette slices for serving

In a spice grinder, pulse together coarse sea salt, dried thyme, and bay leaves to create an herbed salt, 1 to 2 minutes. The granules should have the same consistency throughout. You can also use a mortar and pestle. Generously cover the front and back of duck legs with salt—get all the nooks and crannies. This will add flavor to the duck, but the salt is primarily there to cure the duck legs.

Once generously salted, stack the duck legs in a glass container, cover with a lid, and refrigerate for 12 to 24 hours.

Preheat the oven to 225°F

Rinse the duck legs in cold water to remove salt. Place the legs into a heavy ceramic pot or a deep casserole or baking dish, and cover with duck or chicken stock. Add the peeled garlic cloves, fresh thyme, sliced ginger, and black peppercorns to the pot. Cover the dish or pot, and bake for 4 to 5 hours, until meat is pulling off the bone.

Remove the pot from the oven and, as gently as possible, remove the duck from the fat and jus. Place the duck in a storage container. Strain the fat and jus into a separate tempered glass jar, and allow to come to room temperature. Once the duck meat, fat, and jus reach room temperature, refrigerate for 12 to 24 hours.

Remove the meat and jar of jus and fat from refrigerator. In a medium bowl, separate the duck meat from the bones by finely shredding it with your fingers.

"Well you said you couldn't go out so . . ."
—Ross

"You brought a picnic, ugh, what a boyfriend. That's it, on Monday I start wearing makeup."
—Sophie

The jus and fat should have solidified and separated overnight. Scoop out a spoonful of duck fat from the top of the jar (roughly 2 tablespoons) and place in the bowl with the duck meat. Add in the brandy, mustard, thyme leaves, orange zest, and freshly ground pepper.

Using a hand mixer or stand mixer fitted with the whisk attachment, mix on medium-low speed, until the fat emulsifies with the mustard and the rillette begins to look creamy, 2 to 3 minutes. Slowly add in a spoonful or two of the reserved jus if needed just to help the emulsion come together, and continue to mix for another 1 to 2 minutes.

Once incorporated, firmly press duck rillette into sanitized 4-ounce glass jars with lids. Be sure to press out any air.

Drizzle the rillette with a layer of additional reserved duck fat, a sprinkle of additional orange zest, and a bit of fresh parsley. Cover with lids. While the rillettes can be eaten immediately, it is reccomended you allow it to rest in the refrigerator for 2 to 7 days before serving and it can be kept for at least 2 months if stored properly. Additionally, the remainder of the reserved jus can be used as a stock in another recipe.

Enjoy with crackers or a baguette.

Phoebe's Pregnancy Steak

Season 4, Episode 16
"The One With the Fake Party"

YIELD: 6 servings
PREP AND COOK TIME: 1 hour
INACTIVE TIME: 24 hours

If you're pregnant with your brother's triplets you might be craving steak; if you're just a hungry meat lover like Joey, you also might be craving steak. This recipe is sure to cure any cravings—just keep in mind Phoebe and Joey's pact and help to offset the environmental impact of meat by maybe limiting your consumption. Pair the steak with mocktail The One With the Cat That Doesn't Smell Good (page 174) and Phoebe's Snow Cone Granitas for dessert (page 154).

CHIMICHURRI COMPOUND BUTTER:

1 cup (2 sticks) salted butter, at room temperature
1 shallot, chopped
1 jalapeno, seeded and chopped
4 garlic cloves, crushed
¼ cup parsley, measured and chopped
¼ cup cilantro, measured and chopped
Juice of 1 lime

STEAK:

Six 1½-inch-thick well-marbled rib-eye steaks
¼ cup kosher salt
Arugula for serving
Shaved Parmesan cheese for serving
Lemon wedges for serving

FOR THE CHIMICHURRI COMPOUND BUTTER:

In a food processor, combine everything except the lime juice and pulse until all ingredients are incorporated and the butter looks green, 2 to 3 minutes.

Using a rubber spatula, fold in lime juice in a figure eight motion, so that it isn't sitting on top of the compound butter. Once folded in, give a few pulses, so that the lime juice can incorporate.

Place the compound butter horizontally across a piece of parchment paper. Leave 4 to 5 inches of space on the sides and above the butter. Fold the paper in half with the butter inside, and shape the butter into an even log. Keep the log wrapped in its parchment paper and wrap again in plastic wrap or beeswax paper to keep the butter from tasting like the refrigerator. Place in the refrigerator to allow it to rest overnight and begin preparing the steaks.

Once steaks are done, cut the butter in rounds using a chef's knife dipped in warm water, place rounds of compound butter over each steak. Allow your pregnancy cravings to feel satiated!

NOTES FROM CHEF MONICA:

The rib eye can either be salted just 30 minutes before searing or 18 to 24 hours before searing; anything shorter or longer will cause the salt to pull the juices from the steak, which will result in dry meat. Ideally you should salt for 24 hours, since you have to make a compound butter and it needs time to set anyway.

If you are pregnant or are cooking for someone that is, pick the fattiest well-marbled steak from the bunch, and allow that steak to cook until it is well done, which is about 10 minutes. It is done and safe for pregnant women to eat when it has an internal temperature of 160°F.

FOR THE STEAK:

Place the steaks on a large baking sheet. Salt the steaks on each side with a generous pinch of salt. Be careful not to oversalt. The goal is just to get a light but even coat of salt on both sides of the steak so that it sears beautifully. Cover with a second baking sheet turned upside-down and refrigerate for 24 hours.

At least 30 minutes before cooking, remove steaks from the oven and allow to come to room temperature. Preheat the oven to 500°F.

Heat a large cast-iron skillet on high. Allow the skillet to get so hot that it's almost smoking (you may want to turn your oven fan on). Once hot, working in batches, place the steaks in the skillet. Allow to sear for 1 minute or until the steak begins to pull away from the skillet and then flip and sear on the second side for 1 minute longer. Once seared, set aside on a clean baking sheet, and work on the next batch until all 6 steaks are seared. Reduce the heat to low and allow the empty skillet to remain on the heat in order to stay warm.

Place all 6 seared steaks back into the skillet. (The steaks should not be sitting on top of each other, but it's okay if they are snug.) Season with freshly ground black pepper and place a ½-inch-thick round of compound butter on each steak. Place in oven for 4 to 5 minutes. (You can flip the steaks halfway through, but it's not necessary.)

Remove the steaks from skillet and place on a cutting board. Allow steaks to rest for 4 to 5 minutes before serving.

Once steaks are done, place another round of compound butter over each one, cut steak into slices against the grain, and serve over a bed of arugula and shaved Parmesan. Serve with lemon wedges.

Allesandro's Bouillabaisse

YIELD:
6 servings

PREP AND COOK TIME:
2 hours

When Monica's work at Allesandro's restaurant receives a negative review from a food critic, she becomes quite upset. She shows up at his cooking class to ask him if he'll give her bouillabaisse another shot. When he refuses to change his opinion, Monica's ego is shot. But it seems like the critic's taste buds may be off, this recipe is worthy of five stars.

1 cup mayonnaise

1 teaspoon chili powder

1 garlic clove, grated, plus 2 garlic cloves, finely minced

Salt and pepper

3 tablespoons extra-virgin olive oil

1 large leek, well cleaned and sliced

1 large white onion, diced small

2 fennel bulbs, sliced into thin crescents

½ cup roughly chopped fennel fronds, divided

2 large carrots, diced small

¼ pound cherry tomatoes

1 sourdough batard, cut into 2-inch slices

1 bay leaf

3 tablespoons thyme, chopped

2 tablespoons marjoram, chopped

4 or 5 saffron threads (optional)

1 tablespoon black pepper

9 cups fish stock

2½ cups white wine

Zest and juice of 1 orange

3 pounds cod fillets

2 pounds langoustine, cleaned and halved, or substitute shrimp

½ pound clams, scrubbed

½ pound mussels, scrubbed and debearded

Preheat the oven to 275°F.

In a small bowl, mix together the mayonnaise, chili powder, and grated garlic to make an aioli. Season with salt and pepper to taste, then set aside.

Heat a large stockpot on high. Once hot, reduce heat to medium and add the oil. Once oil is shimmery, about 30 seconds to 1 minute, add the leeks and white onion, and sauté for about 2 minutes. Add the fennel, half of the fennel fronds, and the carrots, and allow to soften, 3 to 4 minutes. Season with salt and pepper.

Once vegetables are soft, add the tomatoes and minced garlic. Stir and allow the tomatoes to break down slightly, about 3 to 5 minutes.

While vegetables cook, toast bread on the middle rack of the oven until golden and slightly crusty, 5 to 7 minutes. Remove the toast from the oven, place in a basket, cover with a towel to keep warm.

Once tomatoes have broken down slightly, add the bay leaf, thyme, marjoram, saffron, and pepper to the mixture. Let simmer 2 to 3 minutes.

Add the fish stock, white wine, and orange zest and juice, and reduce the heat to medium-low. Stir and allow flavors to incorporate, about 3 minutes. Add the thick pieces of cod to the fish stock and cook for 3 minutes, then add the langoustine. Allow langoustine to cook for 1 to 2 minutes before adding the clams and mussels. Cook until the clams and mussels begin to open, 4 to 5 minutes. Turn off heat and cover with a lid. Allow to sit for 2 to 3 minutes before serving. Season with salt and pepper to taste.

To serve, spread an even layer of the aioli over the bread, and ladle generous helpings of bouillabaisse into bowls. Garnish with the remaining fennel fronds and top the bouillabaisse with toast.

Dinner With Friends

The following section features delicious full menu plans with dishes that complement each other and provide a little something for all of your friends.

THE FOOD OF CHANDLER'S ANCESTORS: CHINESE FOOD

Xi'an Lamb Noodles

Shrimp Toast

Spicy Cucumber Salad

Vegetable Fried Rice

FACELESS FOODS

Pumpkin and Cashew Curry

Fried Cauliflower

MONICA'S FRIENDSGIVING FEAST

Roasted Turkey

Mashed Potatoes

Gravy

Cornbread Stuffing

Chandberry Sauce

Winter Salad

Spicy Candied Pecans

Swedish Masseuse Thanksgiving (Vegetarian "Meatballs")

The Food of Chandler's Ancestors: Chinese Food

Joey and Chandler are finally going their separate ways as roommates. Chandler is moving in with Monica, and Joey is becoming an official adult. As a goodbye meal, Joey brings the food of his ancestors, pizza, and suggests that he and Chandler bond one last time over the food of Chandler's ancestors . . . Chinese food?

Xi'an Lamb Noodles

YIELD: 6 servings
PREP AND COOK TIME: 1½ hours
INACTIVE TIME: 4 hours

1 pound lamb shoulder or butt, thinly sliced

⅓ cup dark soy sauce

3 tablespoons rice wine vinegar

2 tablespoons sesame oil

⅓ cup packed brown sugar

1 tablespoon ground cumin

2 tablespoons crushed red pepper flakes

2 garlic cloves, grated

1 teaspoon grated fresh ginger

1½ tablespoons ground Sichuan peppercorn

2 tablespoons cornstarch

One 16-ounce package wide rice noodles or pad see ew noodles

⅓ cup cilantro, roughly chopped for garnish

⅓ cup mint, roughly chopped for garnish

Chile oil (optional)

Spread the lamb slices out on a wooden board. Using a tenderizer or a rolling pin, give the slices a few taps, until each slice is a bit flatter.

In a large bowl, combine the soy sauce, rice wine vinegar, sesame oil, brown sugar, cumin, crushed red pepper flakes, garlic, ginger, Sichuan peppercorns, and cornstarch. Place the lamb in the bowl and use your hands to mix together all the ingredients, turning the lamb so that it is well coated, about 1 minute. Cover and marinate in the refrigerator for 4 hours.

Thirty minutes before serving, pull out the marinated lamb and allow to come to room temperature.

Cook the wide rice or pad see ew noodles according to the package instructions. Drain and set aside.

Heat a wok or large nonstick skillet on high. Once hot, add the lamb slices to the skillet, stirring vigorously. Slowly add in the marinade juice from bowl, and cook until the meat is brown and the sauce is thick, 3 to 5 minutes. Remove from the heat.

To assemble, toss the noodles in the sauce and lamb, turning evenly until the noodles are well coated. Place the noodles on a large serving platter. Garnish with the cilantro and mint. If the lamb is not spicy enough for your taste, drizzle with chile oil.

Shrimp Toast

1 tablespoon coconut oil
½ pound shrimp, peeled and deveined
1 teaspoon minced fresh ginger
¼ cup cilantro
1 garlic clove, minced
1 teaspoon sesame oil
1 egg white
2 large green onions, white and green parts roughly chopped
1 teaspoon sugar
2 teaspoons cornstarch
Salt
4 slices Texas toast bread or thick-cut brioche
⅓ cup sesame seeds, toasted
2 cups peanut oil for frying

In a food processor, combine the coconut oil, shrimp, ginger, cilantro, garlic, sesame oil, egg white, green onions, sugar, cornstarch, and salt to taste. Process until smooth and the ingredients form a paste, 3 to 4 minutes.

Cut the crusts off the bread, and cut each slice in half diagonally to create 8 triangles.

Spread an even layer of shrimp paste onto each triangle.

Sprinkle an even layer of sesame seeds on top of the shrimp paste and bread.

Using a large cast-iron skillet or heavy pan, heat the oil on medium until it reaches 300°F.

Once the oil is hot, reduce the heat to medium-low. Working in batches, place the toasts shrimp-side down into oil, and allow to fry until the sesame is lightly golden and shrimp is pink in color, 1 to 2 minutes. Flip and repeat on the bread side until the toasts are golden brown, 1 to 3 minutes.

Using a slotted spoon, remove the toasts and place on a tray lined with paper towels to drain. Serve immediately.

Spicy Cucumber Salad

YIELD: 6 servings
PREP TIME: 20 minutes

2 large cucumbers
1 tablespoon salt
3 garlic cloves, finely minced
2 tablespoons rice vinegar
1 tablespoon sugar
1 tablespoon sesame oil
1 tablespoon chili garlic paste

Using a rolling pin, lightly smash the cucumber. Cut into 1-inch-thick crescents and place in a colander in the sink.

Sprinkle the cucumber with salt and allow to drain in the colander for 10 minutes.

In a medium bowl, mix together the remaining ingredients, until the sugar and chili paste are dissolved, 1 to 2 minutes.

Mix the salted cucumber into the chili paste mixture, tossing until evenly coated, about 1 minute.

Vegetable Fried Rice

YIELD: 6 servings
PREP AND COOK TIME: 40 minutes

2 tablespoons sesame oil
1 teaspoon grated fresh ginger
2 tablespoons minced shallots
½ head small purple cabbage, shredded
1½ cups broccoli florets
1½ cups medium-diced broccoli stems
½ cup julienned carrots
¼ cup frozen peas
3 tablespoons soy sauce or tamari, divided
3 eggs, beaten (optional)
2 cups day-old cooked jasmine rice
Chile oil (optional)
Green onion, thinly sliced, for garnishing

Heat a large wok on medium-high. Once hot, reduce the heat to medium and add the sesame oil. Allow to heat for 30 seconds to 1 minute, then add the ginger and shallots, until aromatic, about 1 minute.

Next, add the shredded cabbage and toss with the ginger and shallots, until the cabbage breaks down, about 1 minute.

Add the broccoli florets and stems, and carrots, and cook for about 1 minute.

Once vegetables are cooked down, and have a slightly visible char, add the peas and season the vegetables with 1½ tablespoons of the soy sauce or tamari, and allow to cook for about 1 minute.

Push the veggies over to one side of the wok and add the day-old rice. Allow the rice to crisp before stirring, then stir and allow the other side to crisp. Begin to incorporate the vegetables into the rice, and add the remaining soy sauce or tamari to taste.

Push the rice and vegetables over to one side of the wok, and add the eggs, if using. Allow the eggs to sizzle and scramble. Do not mix them with rice until the eggs are mostly cooked through, about 1 minute. Mix in with the rice and vegetables.

For a spicier veggie fried rice, add the chile oil with the eggs or with the soy sauce and rice.

To serve, scoop into bowls and top with sliced green onion.

Faceless Foods

If you're like Phoebe and you don't eat anything with a face (unless you're pregnant with your brother's triplets), try her faceless Fried Cauliflower or Pumpkin and Cashew Curry. These dishes are beautiful, and they're great to serve when having both vegetarian and nonvegetarian friends over for a shared meal.

Pumpkin AND Cashew Curry

1 tablespoon vegetable oil
4 to 6 Thai chile peppers, halved
  (seeded if you want it less spicy)
1½ tablespoons ground turmeric
2 cinnamon sticks
1 teaspoon finely grated fresh ginger
3 pounds Hokkaido pumpkin,
  skinned and cut into 2-inch chunks
2 cups coconut milk
6 to 8 bay leaves
1 cup roasted salted cashews
3 cups cooked basmati rice
1 cup fresh cilantro, measured then
  chopped
Crispy Shallots (page 15)
2 limes, cut into wedges

Place a wok or large sauté pan over medium-high heat with the vegetable oil. Once hot, reduce heat to medium and add the Thai chile peppers, turmeric, cinnamon sticks, and ginger, stirring constantly until the ingredients are aromatic, 2 to 3 minutes.

Add the pumpkin and toss until browned, 3 to 4 minutes.

Reduce the heat to low and add the coconut milk and bay leaves. Allow to simmer for 10 to 12 minutes, until the pumpkin is fork-tender.

Once the pumpkin is cooked, turn off the heat and add the cashews. Allow the cashews to sit in the curry for 3 to 5 minutes. The cashews should be softer, but not mushy. Discard the bay leaves.

To serve, place the cooked rice in a bowl or shallow dish. Top with curry, cilantro, and crispy shallots. Serve with lime wedges.

RECOMMENDED PAIRINGS:
Peanut Butter Fingers Pops for dessert (page 138).

NOTES FROM CHEF MONICA:
Hokkaido pumpkin is an orange winter squash. If you can't find it, you can swap with sugar pumpkins or butternut squash.

Fried Cauliflower

SPICY HARISSA YOGURT:

1 cup full-fat Greek yogurt or labneh
2 tablespoons Marash chile flakes
Juice of ½ lemon
Salt and pepper

GREEN APPLE, CILANTRO, AND LEMON ZEST MEDLEY:

2 green apples, cored, peeled and
   diced small
Juice of ½ lemon
¼ cup cilantro leaves, measured and
   then chopped
1 tablespoon grated lemon zest
Salt and pepper

CAULIFLOWER:

4 cups oil for frying
1 cup cornstarch
½ cup flour
1 teaspoon baking powder
1 tablespoon garlic powder
1 teaspoon dried oregano
1 teaspoon dried thyme
2 tablespoons sesame seeds
1 teaspoon ground sumac
Salt and pepper
1 cup IPA beer or sparkling water
1 large head cauliflower, cut into
   bite-size florets
Cilantro for garnishing

TO MAKE THE SPICY HARISSA YOGURT:

In a small, non-reactive bowl, mix together all the ingredients. Allow to refrigerate for at least 1 hour.

TO MAKE THE GREEN APPLE, CILANTRO, AND LEMON ZEST MEDLEY:

In a small non-reactive bowl, mix together all the ingredients. Allow to refrigerate for at least 1 hour.

Submerge the diced apples in cold water with a squeeze of lemon juice to prevent them from browning.

Drain the apples, pat dry, and toss together with the cilantro and lemon zest in a medium bowl. Season with salt and pepper to taste.

TO MAKE THE CAULIFLOWER:

In a large heavy pot, heat the oil on high to 300°F. Once hot, reduce the heat to medium.

In a large bowl, mix together the cornstarch, flour, baking powder, garlic powder, oregano, thyme, sesame, and sumac. Season with salt and pepper. Next, whisk in the beer or sparkling water, until a batter forms and has no lumps, about 3 minutes.

Working in batches, dip the cauliflower florets into the batter so they're well coated. Shake off any excess batter and place in the oil. Fry until golden, 1 to 2 minutes, then flip and allow to fry an additional 1 to 2 minutes until golden all over. Using a slotted spoon, transfer the fried cauliflower to a serving platter lined with paper towels.

To serve, place the yogurt mixture in a bowl in the middle of a platter and spread the cauliflower around it. Generously top fried cauliflower with the cilantro and green apple medley.

Monica's Friendsgiving Feast

Thanksgiving is always a memorable day on *Friends*. Whether they're playing a very competitive game of touch football, locked out of their apartment because they went up to the roof to see a giant inflatable Underdog escape the Macy's parade route, or making a questionable trifle (Rachel wasn't supposed to put beef in the trifle!), the gang always manages to sit down for a feast. These more traditional recipes are what Monica always *means* to get on the table, even if it doesn't always happen how she planned.

If you buy your turkey frozen, be sure to give it plenty of time to thaw before you cook it. Additionally, remove the neck and giblets from the cavity before beginning this recipe and reserve for the Gravy recipe (page 130).

Roasted Turkey

YIELD: 6 to 10 servings
PREP AND COOK TIME: 8 hours

4 rosemary sprigs, divided, plus more for serving
½ cup fresh sage, divided
½ cup fresh thyme, divided
1 cup (2 sticks) salted butter, at room temperature, divided
4 onions, cut into 3-inch chunks
4 carrots, cut into 3-inch chunks
2 leeks, quartered
Salt and pepper
1 cup white wine
One 12-pound turkey, backbone removed
2 lemons, halved, plus more for serving
2 green apples, cored and quartered
Fresh cranberries for serving
Fresh pomegranates for serving

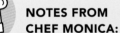

NOTES FROM CHEF MONICA:
Removing the backbone of the turkey or asking your butcher to do so cuts cooking time down and allows for a moister bird.

Preheat the oven to 325°F.

Remove the stems from ¼ cup of the rosemary, ¼ cup of the sage, and ¼ cup of the thyme, then place the leaves in a food processor with 1 stick of the butter. Pulse on high until the herbs are incorporated into the butter.

Place the onions, carrots, and leeks in the bottom of a roasting pan. Season with salt and pepper. Pour the white wine over the vegetables.

Rinse the turkey and pat dry with paper towels. Be sure to disinfect the sink and counter after rinsing the turkey to prevent food-borne illnesses. Place turkey breast-side up on a cutting board. Season the inside of the bird with salt and pepper, then tuck the wings back behind the bird and tie the legs together using food-safe twine. Reform the turkey so that it has somewhat of a cavity.

Place the turkey directly on top of the vegetables, breast-side up. Stuff the cavity with the lemons, apples and the remaining rosemary, sage, and thyme. Season the outside of the bird with salt and pepper.

Using a food-safe brush or your hands, evenly spread the herbed butter over the top of the turkey. Cover the whole pan with aluminum foil and roast for 1 hour and 20 minutes.

After 1 hour and 20 minutes, remove the foil so the skin can become golden brown. If desired, the turkey can be brushed again with the herb butter to baste and aid browning. Continue roasting for an additional 40 minutes to 1 hour, then check the turkey for doneness. Turkey meat should reach an internal temperature of 165°F when measured at the innermost part of the thigh and thickest part of the breast. The meat should no longer be pink and the juices should run clear. If you've removed the backbone from your bird as directed, this could take as little as 2 hours, or as long as 3½ hours if you've left the backbone in. Always check the bird's temperature for safety.

To serve, cover a platter with herbs like sage, rosemary, and parsley. Carefully place the turkey and the contents it was stuffed with in the center of the tray. Place fresh lemon halves, fresh cranberry clusters, or fresh pomegranates torn in half around the platter.

Mashed Potatoes

YIELD: 6 to 10 servings
PREP AND COOK TIME: 40 minutes

4 cups Vegetable Stock (page 14)
or store-bought
3 pounds Yukon gold potatoes,
peeled and cut into 3-inch cubes
2 cups half-and-half
1 or 2 garlic cloves, peeled and
chopped
3 to 5 rosemary sprigs
2 tablespoons unsalted butter
Salt and pepper

In a large pot, combine the vegetable stock, potatoes, and enough water so the potatoes are covered by at least two inches of liquid. Bring to a boil and cook until the potatoes are fork-tender, about 15 minutes. Drain and place in a large bowl.

In a medium pot combine the half-and-half, garlic, and rosemary sprigs. Heat until the mixture is scalding hot but not bubbling over, about 3 minutes. Remove the rosemary and the pour the half-and-half over the potatoes. Mash, removing all lumps and being sure to mash in the garlic. Stir in the butter and season with salt and pepper to taste

To keep warm, the potatoes can be placed in a large metal bowl over a pot filled three-quarters full with steaming water. To lighten Thanksgiving stress, these mashed potatoes can be made up to two days in advance and stored in the refrigerator. To warm, heat over a pot of steaming water. Stir occasionally.

Gravy

YIELD: 6 to 10 servings
PREP AND COOK TIME: 1 hour, 15 minutes

Turkey neck and giblets (optional)
Pan drippings from turkey or ⅓ cup
unsalted butter
½ cup all-purpose flour
8 cups Vegetable Stock (page 14) or
Turkey Stock (page 14)
Salt and pepper

If you're making turkey gravy, in a large pot on medium-high heat, boil the turkey neck and giblets reserved from the Roasted Turkey (page 129). Reduce the heat and allow to simmer for about 1 hour, until the meat is thoroughly cooked.

Remove the meat from liquid, and let cool. Then, use your hands to take the meat off the turkey neck and place in a small bowl. Dice the giblets and set in the bowl with the turkey neck.

Heat a medium pan on medium, and add the pan drippings from the turkey, if you made one, or butter. Allow the drippings to warm or butter to melt before adding the flour, about 1 minute. Stir until a roux forms. Keep an eye on the paste, as it will darken quickly. Cook until the paste is a dark blond color, about 3 minutes.

Add the turkey or vegetable stock, reduce the heat to medium-low, and stir vigorously with a whisk to avoid clumps. Season with salt and pepper to taste.

Cornbread Stuffing

YIELD: 6 to 10 servings
PREP AND COOK TIME: 50 minutes

Cooking spray
1 pound day-old sourdough bread, cut into 1-inch cubes
1 pound cornbread, cut into 1-inch cubes
1 pound Italian sausage, crumbled
1 medium leek, sliced
1 large yellow onion, diced
3 celery stalks, diced small
Salt and pepper
⅓ cup sage, roughly chopped
3 tablespoons rosemary, measured and roughly chopped
3 tablespoons thyme, measured and roughly chopped
2 cups Turkey Stock (page 14)
1 cup apple cider
2 eggs

Preheat the oven to 375°F and coat a large casserole dish with cooking spray.

In a large bowl, place the bread and cornbread croutons.

Heat a large sauté pan on high. Once hot, add in the crumbled Italian sausage and cook until done, about 5 minutes. Remove the sausage with a slotted spoon, leaving behind the fat, and place in the bowl with the croutons.

Place the pan back over medium-high heat, and when the fat is hot, add the leeks, onion, and celery. Sauté until soft, about 5 minutes. Season with salt and pepper to taste.

Pour the vegetables along with the sausage fat over the croutons and sausage. Add the sage, rosemary, and thyme then give it a toss so that croutons are evenly coated with fat and herbs and sausage is well distributed.

In a medium pot on medium heat, heat the turkey stock and apple cider. Once hot, pour over the croutons and toss until the croutons are slightly soggy. Season with salt and pepper to taste.

In a small bowl, beat the eggs with a fork and pour over the stuffing, mixing well. Transfer the stuffing to a 13-by-9-inch baking dish, and bake until top is golden brown, 20 to 30 minutes. If preparing in advance this can be made a day before, and baked 30 minutes before serving.

Chandberry Sauce

YIELD: 6 to 10 servings
PREP AND COOK TIME: 1 hour
INACTIVE TIME: 10 hours

When Chandler finally does come around to celebrating Thanksgiving, he is tasked with making the cranberry sauce, which he quickly turns into the pun "Chandberry Sauce." This sauce should be made the day before.

6 cups cranberries
Zest and juice of 2 oranges
1 cup sugar
2 tablespoons honey (orange blossom honey preferred)
1 cup red wine
1 pinch salt
Freshly ground pepper

In a medium pot over medium heat, combine the cranberries, orange zest and juice, sugar, honey, wine, and salt. Allow to simmer, until the cranberries begin to pop, about 25 minutes. Once the cranberries are popped and begin to thicken, remove from the heat, and allow to cool completely. Refrigerate overnight.

Winter Salad

YIELD: 6 to 10 servings
PREP TIME: 10 minutes

SALAD:

2 pounds arugula

2 small heads radicchio, cut into bite-size pieces

4 crunchy Fuyu persimmons, cut into 1-inch wedges

1 pomegranate, seeded

Spicy Candied Pecans (below)

10 ounces goat cheese

VINAIGRETTE:

⅓ cup maple syrup

Juice of 1 lemon

¼ cup olive oil

1 teaspoon ground cumin

1 teaspoon paprika

2 tablespoons cilantro, roughly chopped

TO MAKE THE SALAD:

Start with a base of arugula and radicchio in a large serving bowl or platter. Top with staggered persimmons, pomegranate seeds, candied pecans, and goat cheese.

TO MAKE THE VINAIGRETTE:

In a small bowl, combine all the vinaigrette ingredients. Whisk vigorously, about 1 minute. Drizzle over the salad just before serving.

Spicy Candied Pecans

YIELD: 2 cups
PREP AND COOK TIME: 20 minutes

2 egg whites

2 cups unsalted pecans

⅓ cup muscovado sugar

1 teaspoon ground cinnamon

1 teaspoon chili powder

Preheat the oven to 250°F and line a baking sheet with parchment paper.

Beat the egg whites in a medium bowl until frothy, about 1 minute.

Add the pecans and coat evenly with the egg whites. Add the sugar, cinnamon, and chili powder, mixing until pecans are evenly coated.

Spread the pecans over the prepared baking sheet and bake until the sugar is bubbly and crisp, 10 to 12 minutes.

Remove from the heat, allow to cool on the countertop, and store in an airtight container for up to 2 weeks. These are great on salads or as snacks.

Swedish Masseuse Thanksgiving

(Vegetarian "Meatballs")

YIELD:
2 to 3 servings

PREP AND COOK TIME:
2 hours

When Rachel receives a gift certificate to a spa franchise, Phoebe makes Rachel promise to never go. She hates corporate massage chains. According to her, "Corporate greed is destroying our hearts and leaving us hollow shells." Of course, Rachel breaks her promise and goes, only to meet a Swedish masseuse who looks oddly (exactly) like Phoebe. But this masseuse's name is Ikea. There's no way Phoebe would work at the corporate massage chain she despises, right? Serve with Chandberry Sauce (page 131).

"MEATBALLS":
½ pound cremini mushrooms, finely chopped
One 15-ounce can cannellini beans, drained
1 small yellow onion, roughly chopped
½ cup Italian bread crumbs
¾ cup panko bread crumbs
2 celery stalks, roughly chopped
½ cup parsley, finely chopped
3 garlic cloves, minced
1 teaspoon vegan Worcestershire sauce
1 tablespoon soy sauce
½ teaspoon liquid smoke
Salt and pepper
Vegetable or canola oil for frying

GRAVY:
2 to 3 tablespoons all-purpose flour
Salt and pepper
1 cup nondairy milk
2 cups Vegetable Stock (page 14) or store-bought
2 tablespoons parsley, roughly chopped, plus more for garnishing
Mashed Potatoes (page 130) for serving

TO MAKE THE "MEATBALLS":
Combine all the "meatball" ingredients except the oil in a food processor. Process until a chunky paste forms, about 2 minutes.

Allow the mixture to sit for about 5 minutes, then roll into 2-inch balls.

Fill a large heavy skillet one-third full with oil and heat on medium-high. Once hot, reduce heat to medium. Working in batches, place 6 to 8 "meatballs" in the pan and allow to brown, 2 to 3 minutes. Then flip to the other side and allow to brown, 2 to 3 minutes more. Transfer the "meatballs" to a plate lined with paper towels to drain and continue browning the rest. Once all "meatballs" are cooked, reserve 2 to 3 tablespoons of oil from the pan.

TO MAKE THE GRAVY:
Heat a large pot on medium. Add the reserved oil from the "meatballs" and the flour. Stir together until a paste forms and turns an amber brown color, 2 to 3 minutes. Season with salt and pepper.

Add in the nondairy milk and stir. The gravy should begin to thicken, 2 to 3 minutes. Season with salt and pepper.

Add the vegetable stock and stir until the gravy is bubbly, 2 to 3 minutes. Reduce the heat to low to keep warm. Season with salt and pepper to taste, and stir in the parsley.

To serve, scoop a generous portion of Mashed Potatoes (page 130) on the bottom of the plate. Top mashed potatoes with 4 to 6 meatballs and gravy. Sprinkle with fresh parsley for garnish.

Sweets and Desserts

Central Perk Almond Biscotti

Peanut Butter Fingers Pops

Kiwi Key Lime Puddin' Cups

Birthday Flan

Central Perk's "Birthday" Muffins

Brown Bird Holiday Macarons

Chocolate Chip Cookies The French Way

Jam-and-a-Spoon Scones

Phoebe's Oatmeal Cookie Ice Cream Sandwiches

Twenty-Year-Old Twinkie

Donut Bread Pudding

The One With the Large Eyebrows on His Hat Cereal Milkshake

Phoebe's Snow Cone Granitas

Little Drops of Heaven Holiday Candy

Bake the Pie . . . Pie

The One With the Large Candy Bar Pie

Blueberry Muffins

Cheesecake Worth Stealing

Rachel's Meat Trifle

Central Perk Almond Biscotti

YIELD: 12 pieces
PREP AND COOK TIME: 1½ hours

Nothing goes better with a cup of Central Perk coffee than these crunchy, lightly sweet biscotti.

1 cup almond flour
1¼ cups all-purpose flour
½ cup sugar
½ teaspoon salt
3 eggs
½ cup olive oil
1 tablespoon almond extract
1 teaspoon grated lemon zest

Preheat the oven to 350°F and line a baking sheet with parchment paper.

In a medium bowl, combine the almond flour, all-purpose flour, sugar, and salt.

In a different medium bowl, combine the eggs, olive oil, almond extract, and lemon zest. Mix into dry ingredients.

On a well-floured surface, roll out the dough into a large rectangle, about 2 to 3 inches thick.

Bake for 30 minutes on the prepared baking sheet, then remove from the oven and allow to cool for 10 minutes.

Transfer the dough to a cutting board and slice the rectangle into cookies that are roughly 1 inch wide. Return the cookies to the prepared baking sheet, cut-side up.

Bake for an additional 15 minutes or until golden brown.

Remove biscotti from the oven, turn over, and bake for an additional 15 minutes, until biscotti is golden.

Peanut Butter Fingers Pops

Season 7, Episode 17
"The One With the
Cheap Wedding Dress"

YIELD: 6 pops
PREP TIME: 20 minutes
INACTIVE TIME: 12 to 24 hours

Who enjoys a spoonful of peanut butter every now and then? I'll tell ya who: Joseph Francis Tribbiani. He makes sure peanut butter fingers—aka two fingers in the peanut butter jar—are even included in Monica's short list of appetizers for her wedding. If you also want two fingers in a jar, but have the dilemma of guests coming over for a shared meal or having to leave the house, try these pops. They're sure to delight and will free up your fingers to do other things like eat Joey's Meatball Sub (page 69).

1 cup smooth peanut butter
1 cup sweetened condensed milk
½ cup full-fat Greek yogurt
1 teaspoon vanilla extract
2 tablespoons honey
Salt
½ cup peanut butter cups,
   dark chocolate chips, or
   roughly chopped pretzels

In a large bowl, combine the peanut butter, sweetened condensed milk, yogurt, vanilla, and honey using a whisk or electric mixer on medium-high speed. Mix until smooth, 2 to 3 minutes.

Place popsicle sticks in six 4-ounce popsicle molds, and pour in the peanut butter mixture. Press a few pieces of chopped peanut butter cups, dark chocolate, or chopped pretzels into the bottom of each pop. Freeze for 12 to 24 hours, and try to keep your fingers out of a peanut butter jar while you wait.

Kiwi Key Lime Puddin' Cups

Season 2, Episode 6
"The One With the Baby on the Bus"

YIELD: 6 servings
PREP AND COOK TIME: 2½ hours
INACTIVE TIME: 4 hours

To celebrate baby Ben's birth, Auntie Monica makes kiwi lime pie. But when the fellas stop over to say hello to Ben and eat a slice, Ross's throat starts to close up. Monica quickly remembers that Ross is severely allergic to kiwi and goes with him to the emergency room. Uncle Joey and Uncle Chandler are left to take care of Ben. When the men discover Ben is the ultimate conversation starter with beautiful women, they take advantage of the opportunity but inadvertently leave him on a city bus. Who knew kiwi lime pie could lead to such chaos? Hopefully this version of Kiwi Key Lime Puddin' Cups brings you lots of luck!

PUDDING:
1½ cups whole milk
1 cup heavy whipping cream
¼ cup cornstarch
1 cup sugar
¼ cup Key lime or lime juice
4 large egg yolks
Zest of ½ lime
2 tablespoons unsalted butter
Pinch of salt
12 graham crackers, crushed
Purple seedless grapes, halved
4 kiwis, peeled and diced

WHIPPED CREAM:
4 cups cold heavy whipping cream
2 tablespoons honey
2 tablespoons mezcal (optional)

TO MAKE THE PUDDING:
In a large saucepan on medium heat, warm the milk and heavy whipping cream until hot but not bubbling, 5 to 7 minutes.

In a large bowl, using a hand mixer on medium-high speed, mix together the cornstarch, sugar, and lime juice. Slowly add in the egg yolks until the mixture is a pale yellow, about 3 minutes.

Using a ladle, slowly drizzle in a ladle's worth of hot milk and cream mixture into the lime and cornstarch mixture while continuously mixing. Mix until the milk is incorporated, 1 to 2 minutes.

Reduce the heat to low and pour the ingredients from the bowl back into the saucepan. Stirring constantly, add the lime zest and butter, one tablespoon at a time, until it has thickened to a pudding consistency, 4 to 5 minutes.

Place pudding in a heat-proof bowl, and cover with plastic wrap. Refrigerate for at least 4 hours.

TO MAKE THE WHIPPED CREAM:
In a large bowl, whip the cold heavy whipping cream and honey until soft peaks form. If you'd like to make it a bit more of an adult dessert, throw in 2 tablespoons of mezcal while whipping.

To serve, place a spoonful of pudding in bottom of a glass jar or glass. Top with crushed graham cracker, grapes and kiwi, and whipped cream. Repeat until glass is three-quarters full. Top with whipped cream and a sprinkle of graham cracker crumbs for garnish.

Birthday Flan

YIELD:
6 servings

PREP AND COOK TIME:
1 hour

Monica plans Rachel's birthday party, but when Rachel's recently divorced parents both show up, chaos ensues. In an attempt to limit the drama, they host two parties, one at Monica's for Rachel's mom, and one at Chandler and Joey's for her dad. Of course, the one at Monica's is boring and stiff, but at least at Monica's there's birthday flan! Woo-hoo!

1½ cups sugar, divided
¼ cup water
3 large whole eggs
2 large egg yolks
Two 14-ounce cans sweetened condensed milk
1 cup whole milk
1 teaspoon vanilla extract

Position a rack in the middle of the oven and preheat the oven to 350°F.

In a medium saucepan on medium-low heat, heat 1 cup of the sugar and water until the sugar is completely dissolved. Gently swirl the pan, until the sugar mixture starts to turn a reddish brown, about 5 minutes.

Pour the caramel mixture into the bottom of a deep 9-inch round baking dish or ceramic tart dish.

In a medium bowl, whisk together the whole eggs, egg yolks, and the remaining ½ cup sugar until well incorporated, 3 to 4 minutes.

In a second medium bowl, mix together the condensed milk, whole milk, and vanilla, while trying to not create a lot of foam.

Pour milk mixture into the egg yolk mixture and stir to combine, again trying to avoid creating bubbles or foam. Gently pour the egg and milk mixture through a sieve and into the baking dish, on top of the caramel mixture.

Place the round baking dish in a deep rectangular baking dish, and pour enough hot water into the rectangular dish to come a quarter of the way up the round dish.

Bake until the center of the flan is gently set, about 40 minutes. Allow to cool at room temperature, then refrigerate overnight.

To serve, gently run a knife around the flan to loosen it from the dish. Turn over onto a plate, and gently shake to release the flan.

Central Perk's "Birthday" Muffins

Season 6, Episode 13
"The One With Rachel's Sister"

YIELD: 24 muffins
PREP AND COOK TIME: 1½ hours

When Joey can't pay for his Central Perk snacks, Gunther offers him a job. In an attempt to flirt with all of the cute female customers, he offers them free muffins on their "birthday." But he soon learns his generosity comes at a price—and that price comes out of his paycheck. These sweet "muffins" are the perfect treat for someone on their birthday.

MUFFINS:
1 cup (2 sticks) unsalted butter
3 cups granulated sugar
3 eggs
2 teaspoons vanilla powder
4 cups cake flour or all-purpose flour
1½ teaspoons baking soda
1½ teaspoon baking powder
2 cups buttermilk
½ cup confetti sprinkles

BIRTHDAY ICING:
1 cup (2 sticks) unsalted butter, softened
7 cups confectioners' sugar
3 tablespoons heavy whipping cream
1 cup jimmies sprinkles, divided

TO MAKE THE MUFFINS:
Preheat the oven to 350°F. Line a cupcake or muffin tin with cupcake cups.

In a large bowl using a hand mixer or using a stand mixer fitted with the paddle attachment, beat the butter and sugar on high until creamed and pale yellow, about 3 minutes.

Beat in 1 egg at a time, making sure each is well incorporated before another.

In a medium bowl, sift together the vanilla powder, flour, baking soda, and baking powder.

Using a spatula and working in small batches, pour in one-third of the dry mixture into the wet mixture. While stirring, add in a splash of buttermilk, and mix. Repeat mixing flour mixture and buttermilk in batches until a batter forms, 3 to 4 minutes.

Stir in the sprinkles. Pour or scoop batter evenly into cups and bake until the cupcakes rise, about 25 minutes. To check for doneness, insert a toothpick into the middle of a cupcake. If the toothpick comes out clean, they're done. If not, continue baking in 5-minute increments until they're done. Allow to cool completely before icing.

TO MAKE THE BIRTHDAY ICING:

In a large bowl, combine the butter and confectioners' sugar. Using a hand mixer or a stand mixer fitted with the whisk attachment, mix the frosting on low until the butter and confectioners' sugar have combined. Then add the heavy whipping cream and vanilla and continue to whip until the frosting is stabilized, about 3 minutes. At this point, add in ½ cup of the sprinkles and mix.

Place the remaining sprinkles on a large plate.

Using a rubber spatula, scoop a generous amount of icing in a heap onto a cupcake. Neatly smooth using the spatula, the roll the icing in the sprinkles, until well coated. You can also use a piping bag fitted with a tip to create a taller layer of frosting, if you'd like.

Brown Bird Holiday Macarons

Season 3, Episode 10
"The One Where Rachel Quits"

YIELD: 20 macarons
PREP AND COOK TIME: 3 hours

When Ross accidentally breaks the leg of a Brown Bird trying to sell enough holiday cookies to make it to space camp, he tries to make it up to the girl by offering to go door-to-door to sell her cookies. Of course, neighbors think he's creepy and slam the door in his face. Luckily, he finds the perfect demographic—college kids suffering from the munchies. These cookies are the perfect gift, treat, or selling point for any bake sale, but if you're not looking for a *baked* sale that sends you to space camp, maybe don't tinker around with the butter in the coconut crème filling, Cookie Duuude.

CHOCOLATE MACARONS:
1⅓ cups finely ground blanched almond flour
2 cups confectioners' sugar
¼ cup unsweetened cocoa powder
½ teaspoon ground cinnamon
3 large eggs, separated for whites, at room temperature
⅛ teaspoon salt

COCONUT CRÈME FILLING:
1 cup (2 sticks) unsalted butter, at room temperature
3 cups confectioners' sugar
1 teaspoon coconut extract
3 tablespoons heavy whipping cream
Salt

TO MAKE THE CHOCOLATE MACARONS:
Line 2 baking sheets with silicone mats. Silicone mats are ideal for making macarons, but parchment paper will do as well.

In a medium bowl, sift together the blanched almond flour, confectioners' sugar, cocoa powder, and cinnamon.

In a large bowl, using a hand mixer or stand mixer fitted with the paddle attachment, beat the room-temperature egg whites and salt at low to medium speed until they start to foam and turn white, 1 to 2 minutes. Once the egg whites are foamy, increase the speed to medium-high and allow to mix until the egg whites become firm and start to shine, 3 to 5 minutes. Soft peaks should begin to form in the meringue.

Working a little at a time, use a rubber spatula to fold the dry ingredients into the meringue. Sprinkle the dry ingredients over the top of meringue and then, using a figure eight motion, gently scoop the top of the egg whites into the bottom of the bowl. Give the bowl a ¼-inch turn every time you scoop. The mixture should begin to look like cake batter. It's okay if the meringue mixture looks a little gloopy and flat. Allow the batter to sit uncovered for 10 minutes.

Using the piping bag method (page 19), place a size 6½ plain tip inside a piping bag or large zip-top bag with a corner cut off, and scoop the macaron mixture into the bag.

Pipe out macarons to about 2 inches in diameter on the prepared baking sheets. Once piped, gently tap the baking sheet on the counter to get rid of any air bubbles in the macarons, and allow to sit for another 30 to 45 minutes. (This helps them to develop their signature outer crust.)

While the macarons are setting, make the coconut crème filling.

When the macarons are done setting, preheat the oven to 350°F.

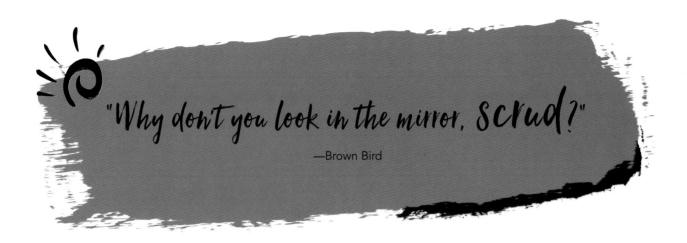

Bake the macarons one sheet at a time for about 10 minutes. Rotate the sheet halfway through the baking time. When done, the tops should be firm, and the bottoms should be crinkly like water-soaked fingertips. Allow to cool completely, 30 to 40 minutes, before filling.

TO MAKE THE COCONUT CRÈME FILLING:
While the macarons set, in a medium bowl, using a hand mixer or a stand mixer fitted with the whisk attachment on low speed, mix together the butter and confectioners' sugar. Once incorporated, mix on a higher speed for 3 to 5 minutes, until the frosting has come together.

Add the coconut extract, heavy whipping cream, and a pinch of salt while still beating, 1 to 2 minutes. The filling is done when the ingredients are well incorporated and the mixture resembles frosting.

Place an open star piping nozzle inside of a piping bag or zip-top bag with a corner cut off, and add the filling.

Gently pipe filling onto the bottom of a macaron, top with another macaron, and set aside. Repeat until all of the macarons are paired.

NOTES FROM CHEF MONICA:
This recipe only uses the whites, but don't throw out the yolks! Save them for another use later.

145

Chocolate Chip Cookies The French Way

Phoebe's French grandma's cookies are a hit! They're so good that the talented Chef Monica begs Phoebe for the recipe. When Phoebe can't find it, they attempt to replicate it and resort to testing the last cookie Phoebe saved in the freezer. Little do they know that the cookies are so famous, the recipe just so happens to be printed on a bag of chocolate chips. You can get that recipe anywhere, so try one of Monica's trial chocolate chip cookie recipes instead.

1 cup (2 sticks) unsalted butter
½ cup granulated sugar
1 cup packed brown sugar
2 whole eggs
1 egg yolk
1 teaspoon vanilla extract
1 teaspoon bourbon (optional)
Zest of ½ orange
2¼ cups all-purpose flour
1 teaspoon baking soda
12 ounces dark (70%) chocolate bar, cut in chunks
Flaky sea salt for sprinkling

In a small pot, melt the butter on medium. Allow to turn brown, about 5 minutes. Keep an eye on the butter, as it can go from melted to burnt quickly. The butter should start to smell nutty and have a brown but clear color to it. Remove the butter from heat, use a rubber spatula to pour the butter and its brown bits into a bowl, and refrigerate until cold, 40 to 60 minutes.

Once the butter is cold, in a large bowl, using a hand mixer on medium speed, mix together the brown butter, granulated sugar, and brown sugar until the mixture becomes pale and almost creamy, 3 to 4 minutes.

Add the eggs and egg yolk, one at a time, mixing for about 20 seconds after each addition.

Add the vanilla, bourbon, if using, and orange zest and mix to combine.

Scrape down the sides of the bowl, and while mixer is on medium low, slowly add in the flour and baking soda. Allow to incorporate, 3 to 4 minutes.

Fold in the chocolate chunks.

Place dough on a clean work surface, divide into quarters, and roll into logs. Wrap in waxed paper or plastic wrap and refrigerate for 1 hour until firm.

Preheat the oven to 350°F and line 2 large baking sheets with parchment paper.

Cut 2-inch-thick discs from the cookie logs and place on the baking sheets 1 to 2 inches apart.

Sprinkle the cookie discs with flaky sea salt and bake for 9 to 10 minutes, until the cookies are lightly golden brown. Eat them with a French accent!

Jam-and-a-Spoon Scones

Season 3, Episode 3
"The One With the Jam"

YIELD: 12 scones
PREP AND COOK TIME: 30 minutes

Joey's a simple guy. When he was a kid his mom would drop him off at the movies with a jar of jam and a spoon, which is very sweet, but impractical. These scones are the perfect vehicle for jam so you *don't* have to eat it alone with a spoon. Serve warm with Lemon Curd (page 13) and The Opposite of Man: Blackberry Mint Jam (page 13) for sweet scones and Tomato Jam (page 74) for savory scones.

2 cups all-purpose flour

½ cup sugar

½ teaspoon salt

2½ teaspoons baking powder

½ cup (1 stick) unsalted butter, frozen and grated with a box grater

½ cup heavy cream

1 large egg

1 teaspoon vanilla extract

Zest of 1 lemon

½ cup goat cheese, crumbled (optional)

2 tablespoons thyme, finely chopped (optional)

Preheat the oven to 350°F and line a baking sheet with parchment paper.

In a large bowl, sift together the flour, sugar, salt, and baking powder. Add the butter, and using your thumb and forefinger, rub butter into the flour, until butter chunks are coated with flour and flat.

In a medium bowl, mix together the heavy cream, egg, vanilla, and lemon zest. Once well combined, pour the wet ingredients into the dry ingredients. Using a wooden spoon or spatula, gently fold together, making a figure eight with the spoon, while you mix.

If you're making a mixture of savory and sweet scones, divide dough in half and add the goat cheese and thyme to the savory dough.

Flour a work surface and your hands. Transfer the dough onto the surface, roll or press the dough out to ¾-inch think, and begin to cut out scones using a cookie cutter or a round dish roughly 2 inches in diameter.

Arrange on the prepared baking sheet, and place in the freezer for 10 minutes.

Remove from the freezer and bake until the scones are fragrant and golden, about 15 minutes.

Phoebe's Oatmeal Cookie Ice Cream Sandwiches

YIELD:
12 sandwiches

PREP AND COOK TIME:
1 hour

There are three things you should know about Phoebe: 1) Her friends are the most important thing in her life; 2) she never lies; and 3) she makes the best oatmeal raisin cookies in the world. Pair those cookies with your favorite ice cream, and you'll discover a fourth truth: Phoebe's ice cream sandwiches are a game changer, especially if you're using them to cushion the blow of having to tell a friend her Italian boyfriend made a pass at you.

1 cup (2 sticks) unsalted butter, softened
½ cup granulated sugar
1 cup brown sugar
1½ teaspoons vanilla extract
2 large eggs
1¾ cups all-purpose flour
1 teaspoon ground cinnamon
1 tablespoon salt
1 teaspoon baking soda
3 cups rolled oats
1 cup raisins
Vanilla ice cream, for serving

Preheat the oven to 375°F. Line a baking sheet with parchment paper.

In a large bowl, mix together the butter, granulated sugar, brown sugar, vanilla, and eggs.

In a medium bowl, mix together the flour, cinnamon, salt, baking soda, rolled oats, and raisins.

Add the dry ingredients to the wet ingredients, and mix thoroughly until a dough forms, about 3 minutes.

Roll or scoop the dough into tablespoon-sized balls and arrange them on the prepared baking sheet. Bake for 10 minutes, until golden and edges are set.

Allow the cookies to rest for a few minutes on the sheet, then transfer to a wire rack to finish cooling.

Once the cookies are cooled, top one cookie with a generous scoop of slightly softened ice cream, then place a second cookie on top. Press gently to create the sandwich, then place on a baking sheet in the freezer to allow the sandwich to firm up a bit more. Repeat with the remaining cookies and ice cream. Allow to chill 15 minutes, then serve.

Twenty-Year-Old Twinkie

Season 2, Episode 16
"The One Where
Joey Moves Out"

YIELD: One 8-inch cake
PREP AND COOK TIME: 1 hour
INACTIVE TIME: 1 to 2 hours

When Monica starts dating Richard (her parents' friend who's twice her age), she becomes the talk of a party at the Gellers' house. "I hear he's got some twenty-year-old Twinkie in the city," one of the guests gossips to Monica's mom. Little do they know that the Twinkie is Monica. The recipe below is a delicious cake that is reminiscent of a Twinkie but provides a fresh dessert to serve at a dinner party.

1 cup polenta
2 cups almond flour
1½ teaspoons baking powder
1¼ cups sugar, divided
3 eggs
1 cup (2 sticks) unsalted butter
Zest of 1 lemon
Juice of 2 lemons
2 tablespoons 20-year-old
   Scotch whisky (optional)
1 cup heavy whipping cream
12 strawberries, sliced

Preheat the oven to 375°F and dust an 8-inch round cake pan with flour.

In a large bowl, stir together the polenta, almond flour, and baking powder.

In a medium bowl, mix together 1 cup of the sugar and the eggs, butter, zest, and lemon juice. Once the mixture is a pale yellow, add to the dry ingredients and stir to combine. Stir in the Scotch whisky, if using.

Transfer the batter into the prepared pan and bake for 25 to 30 minutes, until a toothpick inserted into the middle of the cake comes back dry. If the toothpick comes back with batter, cover with foil and bake for another 5 to 10 minutes. Once the cake is done, allow to cool until it reaches room temperature, 1 to 2 hours.

While cake is baking, allow the remaining ¼ cup sugar to dissolve in the cream in a medium bowl for about 5 minutes.

Using a hand mixer on medium speed, whip the cream until soft peaks form, 5 to 7 minutes.

To serve, cut the cake into slices and top with whipped cream and sliced strawberries.

Donut Bread Pudding

Serve this donut bread pudding for your Friendsgiving Feast (page 126) or holiday party, but you can also take stock in the wise words of Chandler Bing: "Bagels and donuts, round food for every mood." Even if your donuts are a day old, transform this round food into a delicious dessert you can eat whenever your heart desires!

Twelve 1-day-old cake and yeast donuts, cubed
3 egg yolks
½ cup sugar
2 cups whole milk
1 cup heavy cream
1 teaspoon vanilla extract
Zest and juice of 1 lemon
One 8-ounce jar apple butter
One 8-ounce container sour cream

Preheat the oven to 350°F.

Place cubes of donuts in a 10-inch baking dish.

In a medium bowl, mix together egg yolks and sugar until the mixture becomes a pale yellow, about 5 minutes.

In a medium saucepan on medium heat, heat the milk and cream, whisking constantly. Allow the mixture to become scalding hot, 5 to 7 minutes.

Begin whisking the egg mixture. While whisking, pour ¼ cup of the milk and cream mixture into the egg mixture. Mix until well incorporated to temper.

Once incorporated, pour the tempered egg mixture into milk mixture, stirring, and return to medium-low heat to create a crème anglaise. Add the vanilla extract, zest, and juice, and allow the mixture to thicken, 5 to 10 minutes.

Pour the crème anglaise over the donuts and gently toss with your hands, making sure the donut cubes are evenly coated, and bake until golden brown, about 25 minutes.

Serve with dollops of apple butter and sour cream.

The One With the Large Eyebrows on His Hat Cereal Milkshake

YIELD:
2 large milkshakes

PREP TIME:
20 minutes

INACTIVE TIME:
2 hours

What's weirder? That the Cap'n on a cereal box has eyebrows on his hat or that he's been the captain of a cereal for more than forty years? I don't know, but I do know that these milkshakes are a completely different level of satisfaction.

CANDY-GLAZED STRAWBERRIES:
6 large strawberries
1 cup sugar
¼ cup water

MILKSHAKES:
⅓ cup frosting
1 cup sugary cereal, divided
8 miniature frozen waffles
    for garnishing
6 miniature sausage patties
    for garnishing
6 scoops vanilla ice cream
1¼ cups whole milk
¼ cup jimmies sprinkles, plus more
    for garnishing
Whipped cream for topping

TO MAKE THE CANDY-GLAZED STRAWBERRIES:

Skewer three of the strawberries so that the greens are facing up and arrange them so they are at the edge of the skewer. Repeat with other three strawberries. Be sure the strawberries are completely dry. Prepare a drying station by either setting a block of Styrofoam nearby or lining a baking sheet with parchment paper.

In a medium pot, place the sugar and water on high heat. Bring to a boil and cook until the syrup reaches 300°F on a candy thermometer, or the hard candy stage. Once the syrup is hot, dip the strawberries in and twist.

Stick the skewers in Styrofoam to let dry upright, or lay them on the prepared baking sheet, and allow to dry for at least 2 hours.

TO MAKE THE MILKSHAKES:

Using a rubber spatula, spread frosting on the outside rims of milkshake glasses. Push half of the sugary cereal on the icing so it sticks to the glass. Allow to set in the fridge for at least 1 hour.

Toast the miniature waffles according to the package instructions.

Heat a small pan on high. Once hot, reduce the heat to medium and add the sausage patties. Once the patties start to brown, flip and cook for about 2 minutes longer. Remove sausages from heat and create a sandwich by alternating pieces of waffle and sausage until you have a mini sandwich 6 tiers high. Skewer the waffle sandwich and repeat with the remaining waffles and sausages. Set aside.

In a blender, place the ice cream, milk, and the remaining cereal. Blend until smooth and frothy, about 3 minutes.

Place half the jimmies sprinkles in the bottom of each frosted glass. Pour the ice cream into the glasses and top with whipped cream. Place a dried candy-glazed strawberry skewer and waffle skewer on the side of each milkshake glass and serve immediately.

Phoebe's Snow Cone Granitas

In true Monica fashion, she takes control of planning Rachel's birthday party. When Phoebe is relegated to being in charge of bringing cups and ice, she decides she's going to make it the best ice party Rachel has ever seen. She gets crushed ice, cubed ice, and fancy dry ice. She even creates an ice cup hat. Want to try your hand at creativity and ice? These snow cone granitas are just the ticket.

One 10-pound seedless watermelon
Juice of 3 limes
1½ cups sugar
One 8-ounce can sweetened condensed milk for serving (optional)

Scoop the flesh of the watermelon into a food processor or blender. Puree until smooth.

In a large bowl, stir together the watermelon juice, lime juice, and sugar. Pour into a rimmed baking sheet and freeze for 1 hour.

Using a fork, comb through the ice, breaking it up, and put back into the freezer. Freeze for another hour. Repeat the process until liquid is slushy and frozen, 3 to 4 hours.

To serve, scoop a desired amount into a red plastic cup and top with a drizzle of sweetened condensed milk.

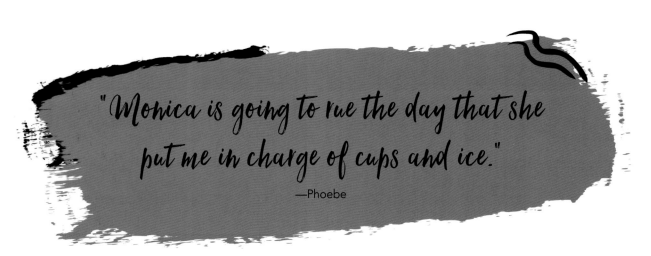

"Monica is going to rue the day that she put me in charge of cups and ice."

—Phoebe

Litttle Drops of Heaven Holiday Candy

Monica tries to get to know her neighbors better by making candy for the building, but when the candy becomes a hot-ticket item, neighbors begin to riot outside of her apartment for more. They're so good that one guy even describes them as "little drops of heaven" when he's standing at Chandler and Monica's door at 4 a.m. asking for more, so be careful who you hand these babies out to.

½ cup (1 stick) butter, cut into pieces, plus more for the pan
1½ cups sugar
1¼ cups goat milk
1¼ cups heavy cream
Flaky sea salt for sprinkling

Set a large pot over medium-high heat and add the butter, sugar, goat milk, and heavy cream.

Stir the mixture constantly while keeping the candy thermometer partly submerged in it. When the temperature reaches 250°F, immediately remove the pot from the heat.

Butter a baking sheet, and spread the caramel over it. Sprinkle with sea salt, and allow to set. Once cool, cover and refrigerate overnight until caramel becomes firm.

Cut waxed paper into 3-by-3-inch squares.

Using a wet knife, cut the caramel into squares and wrap in waxed paper. Twist the waxed paper on both ends to form candy wrappers.

NOTES FROM CHEF MONICA:
Goat milk may not be easy to find, but it is necessary to create this incredibly complex and delicious caramel.

Bake the Pie . . . Pie

YIELD:
1 pie

**PREP AND
COOK TIME:**
45 minutes

Rachel accidentally leaves the hair straightener on at Phoebe's place and catches the whole apartment on fire. Sadly, both girls find themselves in need of a new living arrangement. Rachel stays at Joey's and Phoebe ends up staying in Monica's new guest room where she is waited on hand and foot. "Does that smell bother you?" Monica asks Phoebe of an odor wafting over from across the hall. "Just let me know and I can bake a pie to cover it." But no one needs an excuse to bake a pie. Cherries and coffee are an unlikely but wonderful combination. Coffee smooths out the tart undertones of the cherries, and the cherries perk up the chocolatey notes of coffee.

Two 14.5-ounce cans red tart cherries
2 tablespoons instant coffee
½ cup sugar
2 tablespoons cornstarch
1 recipe Pie Crust dough (page 12), divided

Preheat the oven to 375°F.

In a medium pot, combine the cherries, instant coffee, and sugar. Heat on medium, stirring occasionally, until the sugar is dissolved and coffee is well incorporated, about 5 to 7 minutes. Reduce the heat and allow to simmer.

Spoon 2 or 3 spoonfuls of cherry juice from the pot into a small bowl. Add the cornstarch and whisk vigorously making sure that no lumps form. Pour the cornstarch mixture back into the pot of cherries, and allow to simmer, stirring, until the cherry mixture thickens, about 5 minutes. Remove from the heat and set aside.

On a well-floured, nonporous surface, roll out half of the pie crust dough so it is larger than a 9-inch pie dish. Carefully transfer the dough into the pie dish. Pour in the cherry mixture.

Roll out the second pie crust and top the pie however you would like. One option is to roll out the second half of the dough into a single sheet and top the pie with the second crust, trim the edges and then crimp the crusts together. Cut three sizeable slits in the top of the pie, so that steam escapes while it bakes. Alternatively, you can create a lattice pattern by slicing the second pie crust into long strips and weaving them together.

Place the pie on the middle rack of the oven and bake until the crust is golden, 20 to 30 minutes.

Allow to cool to room temperature before serving.

The One With the Large Candy Bar Pie

Season 4, Episode 17
"The One With the Free Porn"

YIELD: 6 servings
PREP AND COOK TIME: 1 hour
INACTIVE TIME: 6 to 8 hours

When Ross goes to the airport to tell Emily he loves her, she hands him a rather large candy bar. "Here, have this," she says. "I'm only allowed one piece of carry-on anyway." Later, when she comes back to the States to confess her love for Ross, she brings the same large candy bar. Joey can't help but be smitten. He's never seen such a big candy bar. This recipe combines Joey's first love, food, and Ross's sad love life, costarring in "The One With the Large Candy Bar Pie."

1½ cups crushed graham crackers
6 tablespoons (¾ stick) unsalted butter, at room temperature
6 ounces baking chocolate
27 ounces Swiss chocolate candy bars with nougat, almonds, and honey, separated into pieces
1 cup heavy cream

In a large bowl, mix together the graham cracker crumbs and butter until they begin to stick together, 3 to 4 minutes.

Transfer the mixture into a 9-inch pie dish. Using your hand or the bottom of a glass, firmly and evenly press the mixture into the bottom and sides of the pie dish. Be sure to press the crust evenly around the edges. Cover and refrigerate for 2 to 4 hours.

Create a double boiler by placing a medium pot filled halfway with water on medium heat. Once the water starts to steam, place a metal bowl on top of the pot. Add the baking chocolate and about 10 ounces of the chocolate candy bars to the bowl. Stir constantly and allow chocolate to melt. Once chocolate is melted, add the cream, stirring vigorously, and remove from the heat.

Pour the chocolate mixture into the cold pie crust, and refrigerate for about 4 hours, until the filling is firm.

Once the chocolate is firm, place additional chocolate bar pieces in concentric circles on top of the pie to decorate.

NOTES FROM CHEF MONICA:
A double boiler helps melt ingredients like chocolate over indirect heat.

Blueberry Muffins

When Rachel asks Ross to bring her a muffin from the coffeehouse, he asks her which kind she'd like, and she stops and thinks very hard about what she wants. After all, it's an important decision. Not like, say, deciding to marry someone. This is about a *muffin*. When you make these muffins at home, you can rest assured that blueberry is always the right answer.

2 cups all-purpose flour
1 cup coarse cornmeal
4 teaspoons baking powder
1 teaspoon salt
2 eggs
½ cup coconut oil or unsalted butter, softened
Zest and juice of 1 small lemon
1 cup milk
2 cups blueberries
⅓ cup sparkling coarse sugar (optional)

Preheat the oven to 350°F. Line cupcake or muffin tins with cupcake liners.

In a medium bowl, sift together the flour, cornmeal, baking powder, and salt.

In a second medium bowl, using a hand mixer or whisk, mix together the eggs, oil, lemon zest, lemon juice, and milk.

Add the wet mixture to the dry mixture, stirring until the batter has no clumps, 3 to 4 minutes. Fold in the blueberries.

Using an ice cream scoop, scoop batter into the cupcake cups.

Top each cupcake with sparkling sugar and place in the middle rack of the oven. Bake until the muffins rise and are golden brown, 20 to 25 minutes.

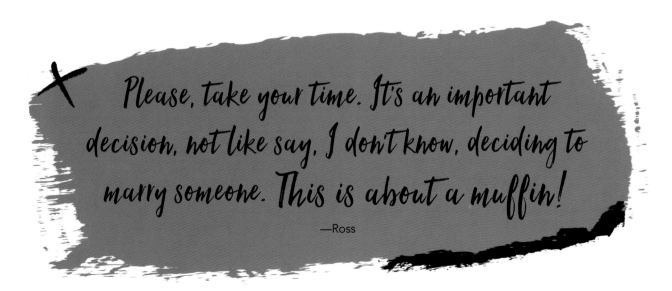

Please, take your time. It's an important decision, not like say, I don't know, deciding to marry someone. This is about a muffin!

—Ross

Cheesecake Worth Stealing

Season 7, Episode 11
"The One With All the Cheesecakes"

YIELD: 1 cheesecake
PREP AND COOK TIME: 1½ hours
INACTIVE TIME: 8 to 10 hours

You have got to try this cheesecake, even if you don't have much of a sweet tooth—as Rachel claims. While it may not be the one from Mama's Little Bakery, you'll have all your friends saying, "Wow, my god, so creamy!" before you know it with this recipe. With a "buttery, crumbly graham cracker crust with a very rich, yet light cream cheese filling," this cheesecake will be a huge hit at your next gathering. Maybe just don't eat it off the floor like Rachel and Chandler do.

CRUST:
1 cup crushed honey graham cracker crumbs (about 5 crackers)
¼ cup (½ stick) unsalted butter, melted, plus more for the pan
2 tablespoons sugar
¼ teaspoon freshly grated nutmeg
½ cup walnuts, pecans, or almonds

FILLING:
2 pounds cream cheese, at room temperature
1 cup sugar
3 large eggs, at room temperature
2 vanilla beans, split lengthwise and scraped
Juice of 1 lemon, strained
2 teaspoons vanilla extract

TOPPING:
2 cups sour cream
¼ cup sugar
1 vanilla bean, split lengthwise and scraped

TO MAKE THE CRUST:
Position a rack in the middle of the oven and preheat the oven to 350°F. In a food processor or blender, combine the cracker crumbs, butter, sugar, nutmeg, and nuts. Process until mixed thoroughly.

Butter the bottom and sides of a 9-inch springform pan. Pour the crumb mixture into the pan and, using your hand or the bottom of a glass, press it evenly into the pan bottom. Bake the crust until it is a little bit darker brown and smooths out, 10 to 12 minutes. Leave the crust in the springform pan and transfer to a wire rack and let cool completely.

TO MAKE THE FILLING:
Reduce the oven to 325°F. Line a baking sheet with parchment paper.

In a large bowl, using a stand mixer fitted with the paddle attachment or a hand mixer, mix the cream cheese on low speed until creamy. Add the sugar and mix slowly until smooth. Turn off the mixer and scrape down the bowl and beater with a rubber spatula. On low speed, add the eggs one at a time, beating gently after each addition. Scrape down the bowl again.

Add the vanilla beans, lemon juice, and vanilla extract. Mix again on the lowest speed until smooth and creamy. It is important to whip as little air into the mixture as possible to prevent the cheesecake from sinking in the middle once it is baked.

Place the cooled crust on the prepared baking sheet and pour the filling into the crust. Cover the cake pan with a pot lid or another sheet pan to insulate the cake while it bakes. Bake the cheesecake until the center jiggles very slightly when the pan is gently shaken, 45 to 50 minutes.

If the center looks soupy, re-cover the cheesecake and continue to bake for a few more minutes.

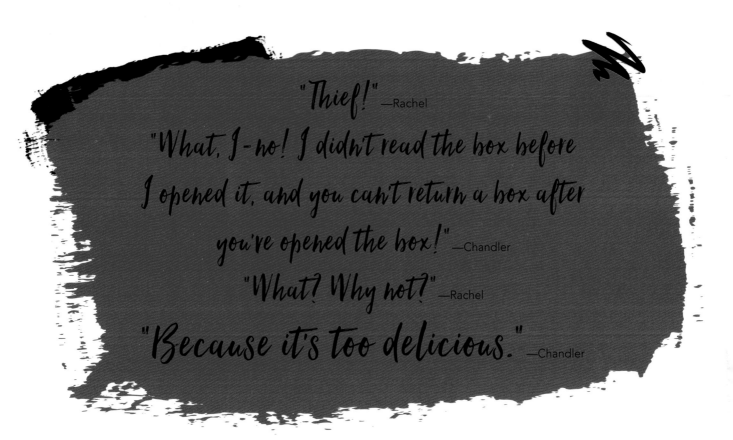

"Thief!" —Rachel

"What, I—no! I didn't read the box before I opened it, and you can't return a box after you've opened the box!" —Chandler

"What? Why not?" —Rachel

"Because it's too delicious." —Chandler

TO MAKE THE TOPPING:

While the cheesecake bakes, make the topping. In a small bowl, combine the sour cream and sugar. Add the vanilla bean and stir well. Cover with plastic wrap and set aside at room temperature until needed.

Remove the cheesecake from the oven and uncover it. Carefully pour the topping around the edge of the cheesecake. Using a small offset spatula, gently spread the topping out evenly over the entire surface of the hot cheesecake. Do not press down too hard, or the topping will sink into the cake.

Re-cover the cheesecake, return it to the oven, and bake for another 5 minutes just to set the topping. Transfer the cheesecake to a rack and let cool at room temperature, covered, for 1 to 2 hours. Remove the lid or sheet pan. Cover the cooled cheesecake with a 10-inch cardboard circle covered with plastic wrap or with a large, flat plate. Refrigerate overnight.

To unmold, set the cheesecake on a tall, narrow can or on a bowl. Release the pan sides, opening them widely so that they fall away from the cake. Set the cheesecake on a serving plate and serve cold. Store in an airtight container in the refrigerator for up to 5 days.

F·R·I·E·N·D·S

Rachel's Meat Trifle

Season 6, Episode 9
"The One Where Ross Got High"

YIELD:
1 large trifle

PREP AND COOK TIME:
50 minutes

You won't need impromptu acting classes from Joey to pretend that this meat trifle is delicious. You also won't need to eat it on the balcony alone, where you'll claim a bird swooped in to steal it, or in the bathroom while you look at yourself in the mirror. In fact, you'll probably be begging for a second helping as the sweet and savory flavors of the candied bacon work together beautifully—much better than Rachel's half an English trifle and half a shepherd's pie.

5 or 6 slices thick-cut applewood-smoked bacon
¼ cup packed brown sugar
2 cups heavy whipping cream
3 cups Lemon Curd (page 13)
2 pounds pound cake, cut into 2-inch cubes
1 cup The Opposite of Man: Blackberry Mint Jam (page 13)
Strawberries, quartered
Blueberries

Preheat the oven to 350°F. Line a baking sheet with parchment paper and place a baker's rack on top.

Place the bacon horizontally across the baker's rack and coat with the brown sugar, being sure to cover thoroughly. Bake until the bacon is crispy and the sugar has candied, about 20 minutes. Remove from the oven and set aside.

In a large bowl, using a hand mixer on medium-high speed, whip the cream until stiff peaks form, about 5 minutes.

Using a rubber spatula, gently fold the lemon curd into the whipped cream.

Begin to layer a trifle dish with a layer of pound cake, dollops of jam, and berries, then top with the whipped cream and lemon curd. Repeat until the final layer is whipped cream and lemon curd.

Cut the candied bacon into bite-size pieces and place on top of the trifle.

Drinks

Gunther's Cold Brew

Rachelrita

Tiki Death Punch

Miss Chanandler Bong

Ross's 72 Long-Stemmed Rose Tea

Regina Phalange

The Official Rulebook of Fireball

The Ross-a-Tron

The One With the Cat That Doesn't Smell Good

Milk Master 2000

The Geller Cup

Gunther's Cold Brew

Season 6, Episode 9
"The One Where Ross Got High"

YIELD:
6 servings

PREP TIME:
10 minutes

INACTIVE TIME:
12 hours

Outside of his undying love for Rachel and his crazy hair, we know Gunther as the manager of Central Perk, and we can all probably assume he'd be very into cold brew coffee to keep him going during those long coffeehouse shifts.

1 cup coarsely ground coffee beans
4 cups cold water
Cream or whole milk (optional)

Combine the ground coffee and water in a pitcher. Allow to sit for up to 12 hours. Strain through a coffee filter.

To serve, fill a glass with ice. Fill halfway with water. Fill the remainder of the glass with cold brew coffee.

Add milk or heavy cream to taste, if desired.

Rachelrita

One of the great things about living across the hall, or across the street, from your best friends is that when you don't have all the ingredients you need to make margaritas, someone else probably does.

¾ ounce triple sec
1 ounce grapefruit juice
1 ounce mezcal
1 ounce tequila
Prosecco
Grapefruit peel for garnishing

Measure the triple sec, grapefruit juice, mezcal, and tequila into a shaker with ice. Shake for 10 seconds to 15 seconds and strain through a tea strainer into a glass. Top with a splash of prosecco. Garnish with a dramatic long piece of grapefruit peel.

SERVICE

Tiki Death Punch

On that fateful night when the girls are misdelivered a pizza meant for G. Stephanopoulos (page 81), they've already gotten the party started with Monica's Tiki Death Punch.

2 ounces heavy cream
3 ounces simple syrup
4 ounces lime juice
8 ounces soda water
20 fresh or frozen strawberries, plus more for garnishing
Ice

Combine the heavy cream, simple syrup, lime juice, and soda water in a blender and add the strawberries. Blend with a few pieces of ice and pour into glasses. Garnish with half a strawberry wedged on the side of each glass and a fun straw if you like. Drink with friends while spying on George Stephanopoulos.

For a boozier version, add 8 ounces rum and 6 dashes Peychaud's bitters.

Miss Chanandler Bong

Every week the *TV Guide* comes to Joey and Chandler's apartment. What name appears on the address label? In a trivia game between the girls and the boys with their apartments on the line, Rachel gets a little ahead of herself, proudly yelling, "Chandler gets it! It's Chandler Bing!" But of course, that would be a little too easy.

¾ cup water
¾ cup granulated sugar or demerara sugar
5 cinnamon sticks
1 egg white
½ ounce lemon juice
1½ ounces pineapple juice
1 to 2 ounces ginger beer
Ground cinnamon for garnishing

In a small pan, bring the water to a boil. Add the sugar and simmer until dissolved. Add 5 cinnamon sticks to the mixture and simmer for 15 minutes. Turn off the heat and allow to infuse for 30 minutes. Remove the cinnamon sticks. The syrup can be kept for up to a week in a refrigerator.

Add to a shaker the egg white, lemon juice, 1 ounce of the cinnamon simple syrup, and the pineapple juice. Shake without ice for 15 to 20 seconds. Add ice and shake vigorously for another 15 seconds.

Strain through a tea strainer into a coupe glass and top with the ginger beer. Add a dash of cinnamon across the top of the cocktail for garnish.

For a more adult treat, add 2 dashes angostura bitters and 1½ ounces scotch whiskey to the shaker. Use just 1 ounce pineapple juice. Add an extra ounce of ginger beer on top. Garnish with a pineapple wedge if desired.

Ross's 72 Long-Stemmed Rose Tea

YIELD: 1 serving
PREP TIME: 40 minutes

In an effort to make amends with his wife Emily for accidentally calling her Rachel at the altar, Ross sends her 72 long-stemmed red roses, one for every day he's known and loved her. She sends them back mulched up in a box, so this drink will help drown his sorrows.

1 cup water
1 cup sugar
4 chamomile tea bags
½ ounce rose water
2 ounces juniper and Inca berry nonalcoholic spirits, or other store-bought botanical nonalcoholic infusions
Dried rose petals for garnishing

In a small pan, bring the water to a boil and then add the sugar, boiling until dissolved. Add the chamomile tea bags and allow to simmer for 15 minutes. Turn off the heat and infuse for an additional 20 minutes. Strain.

In a mixing glass combine ½ ounce of the chamomile simple syrup, the rose water, and the nonalcoholic spirits. Stir for 10 to 15 seconds and strain into a Nick and Nora glass with a julep strainer. Garnish with a dried rose petal.

To make an adult version of this drink, omit the nonalcoholic spirits and add ½ ounce gin and 1 ounce vodka.

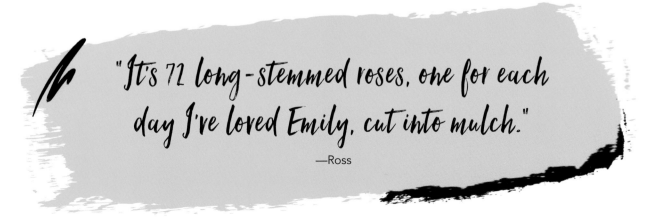

"It's 72 long-stemmed roses, one for each day I've loved Emily, cut into mulch."

—Ross

Regina Phalange

Whenever Phoebe needs an alias, Regina Phalange is right there in her back pocket.

BLACK PEPPER HONEY SYRUP:
½ cup water
½ cup honey
1 teaspoon black peppercorns or coarsely ground black pepper

6 ounces coconut water
3 tablespoons coconut cream
½ teaspoon golden milk powder or ground turmeric
Freshly ground black pepper for garnishing

TO MAKE THE BLACK PEPPER HONEY SYRUP:
Place a small saucepan over medium-high heat. Bring the water to a simmer, add the honey, and stir.

Reduce the heat to medium-low, and while the water and honey continue to warm, crush 1 teaspoon of black peppercorns into rough pieces in a mortar and pestle or spice grinder. If using coarsely ground black pepper, simply add to honey mixture. Continue to simmer on low heat for 10 minutes, being careful not to let the mixture caramelize. Turn off heat and infuse for another 20 minutes. Strain off the black pepper pieces.

TO ASSEMBLE:
Place a small saucepan over medium heat. Add the coconut water and bring to a simmer. Add the coconut cream and whisk together while heating.

Add golden milk powder or ground turmeric, then add 1 ounce of the black pepper honey syrup and continue to warm until the mixture simmers. Warm for 1 minute and strain the entire mixture through a tea strainer into a mug. Garnish with a grind of black pepper on top.

The Official Rulebook of Fireball

Season 5, Episode 2
"The One With All the Kissing"

YIELD: 2 servings
PREP AND COOK TIME: 30 minutes

When Joey is supposed to be writing a script for himself to play the lead in, he finds something much more fun—and dangerous—to write instead: the rule book for his new favorite game.

3 ounces water
3 ounces honey
½ teaspoon cayenne pepper, plus more for garnishing
1½ ounces apple cider vinegar or switchel
13½ ounces apple cider

Bring the water to a simmer in a small pan and add the honey. Add the cayenne pepper to the liquid and simmer for 1 minute. Turn off the heat and allow to infuse for 20 minutes. Strain off the cayenne.

In a small saucepan, warm the cayenne-honey syrup, apple cider vinegar or switchel, and apple cider together until steaming but not boiling. Divide into two mugs and garnish with a sprinkle of cayenne pepper over the top to taste.

The Ross-a-Tron

Season 7, Episode 11
"The One With All the Cheesecakes"

YIELD: 1 serving
PREP TIME: 5 minutes

Ross is always trying to make himself seem way cooler than he is. Shocking that the nickname Ross-a-Tron never caught on.

1 egg
½ ounce simple syrup
½ ounce lemon juice
½ ounce bourbon
1 ounce amaretto liqueur
Crushed graham crackers for serving

In a shaker combine the egg, simple syrup, lemon juice, bourbon, and amaretto liqueur. Add a single ice cube and shake for 10 to 15 seconds. Add a scoop of ice to the shaker tin and shake for another 15 to 20 seconds. Double strain into a martini glass. Sprinkle crushed graham crackers in a line across the top of the cocktail.

173

The One With the Cat That Doesn't Smell Good

It's not your fault, cat.

½ ounce simple syrup
¾ ounce lemon juice
1½ ounces distilled nonalcoholic spirit
1½ ounces diet cola

Add to a shaker the simple syrup, lemon juice, and non-alcoholic spirit. Shake with ice and strain into a highball glass filled with ice and top with diet cola. Garnish with a fun straw.

To make it boozy, replace the nonalcoholic spirit with 1½ ounces bourbon.

Milk Master 2000

What kind of idiot can't pour milk? Joey—when he's trying to film an infomercial for the Milk Master 2000.

1 scoop vanilla ice cream
   (or vanilla soy ice cream if it's not a serious breakup)
½ ounce cold brew coffee syrup
   (store-bought)
½ ounce chocolate syrup
Coffee bean for garnishing

In a shaker, combine the ice cream, cold brew coffee syrup, and chocolate syrup. Shake without ice and strain into a coupe glass. Garnish with a coffee bean grated over top with a zester.

For a more adult version, replace the chocolate syrup with crème de cacao.

The Geller Cup

The Gellers are very competitive, even when what they're competing for is a troll doll nailed to a two-by-four.

1 medium sweet potato
1 egg white
½ ounce maple syrup
3 ounces orange juice
3 marshmallows, toasted over an open flame, for garnishing

Preheat the oven to 350°F and roast a sweet potato for 45 minutes. Stick a fork in the potato and if it goes in easily, it's done, otherwise roast longer. Allow to cool fully. Peel and discard the skin, then mash the flesh with a potato masher.

Add a heaping tablespoon of mashed sweet potato purée to a shaker, along with the egg white, maple syrup and orange juice. Shake with a single ice cube for 10 seconds to emulsify the egg white. Add more ice and shake for another 10 to 15 seconds. Strain into a rocks glass and top with ice. Garnish with three marshmallows that have been toasted over an open flame.

INSIGHT EDITIONS

PO Box 3088
San Rafael, CA 94912
www.insighteditions.com

 Find us on Facebook: www.facebook.com/InsightEditions

 Follow us on Twitter: @insighteditions

Published by Insight Editions, San Rafael, California, in 2020.

No part of this book may be reproduced in any form without
written permission from the publisher.

Library of Congress Cataloging-in-Publication Data available.

ISBN: 978-1-64722-343-4

Publisher: Raoul Goff
President: Kate Jerome
Associate Publisher: Vanessa Lopez
Creative Director: Chrissy Kwasnik
VP of Manufacturing: Alix Nicholaeff
Designer: Leah Lauer
Senior Editor: Amanda Ng
Editorial Assistant: Anna Wostenberg
Managing Editor: Lauren LePera
Production Editor: Jennifer Bentham
Production Director/Subsidiary Rights: Lina s Palma
Production Manager: Eden Orlesky

Insight Editions, in association with Roots of Peace, will plant two
trees for each tree used in the manufacturing of this book. Roots
of Peace is an internationally renowned humanitarian organization
dedicated to eradicating land mines worldwide and converting
war-torn lands into productive farms and wildlife habitats. Roots
of Peace will plant two million fruit and nut trees in Afghanistan
and provide farmers there with the skills and support necessary
for sustainable land use.

Manufactured in China by Insight Editions

10 9 8 7 6 5 4 3 2

Dedication: For Mozes, Storm, and Michel.

Acknowledgements:
To: Amaluz, Sam Saraf, Martine, Amanda Lopez, Soleil Ho, Celeste,
Shakirah Simley, Vinny, Ohn, Zozo, Victor (The Uno Champ), Rasmus
Ege, and Bougie, your generosity, love, humor, and hospitality were
instrumental in seeing me through to the finish line on this project. If I
had my own sitcom about a group of amazing friends, you'd all be in it.
I love you guys! Tusind Tak!

To: Bryant Terry, your care, commitment to excellence, mentorship,
and space in my life is everything. Thank you for being an amazing big
brother, friend, employer, and James Brown to my Bobby Byrd.

To: Dad. You have always been the first step in my culinary journey.
Thank you for teaching me how to make French toast, and thank you
for allowing me to make you the most disgustingly piquant sandwich I
could muster at the age
of three.

To: Mom, the funniest lady in showbiz. Thank you for being an artist,
which inspired me to be creative. Thank you for being my Mom-
therapist when I would call in the wee hours with endless worries and
complaints. I love you.

To: My amazing team. Thank you Koren, for your amazing, professional,
and hard work on this project. Your kindness and positive attitude
was the glue that kept us going. Thank you Mary, for your greatness,
expertise, and recipe development for the drink portion of this book!
Thank you Brenna! You're the hardest shopper of props, groceries, and
backdrops out there. Dorothy Faye! Woo, girl! You're my godsend. I
love you and am so thankful you miraculously showed up to salvage,
create, and wash dishes. I owe you. And thank you to you sexy models
on the first day of the shoot! You all set the precedent for an excellent
project and great cookbook!

To: Jolene. You're an amazing tracker. I don't even know how to begin
to thank you enough.

To: My editor, Amanda Ng. Thank you for your editorial and publishing
brilliance, for going the extra mile, and for being another great Amanda
in the sea of great Amandas.